RECORDED VERSIONS
GUITAR
AUTHENTIC TRANSCRIPTIONS
WITH NOTES AND TABLATURE

The Jimi Hendrix Experience
axis:
bold as
love

ISBN 978-0-7935-2391-7

EXPERIENCE
HENDRIX
"A JIMI HENDRIX FAMILY COMPANY"

EXCLUSIVELY DISTRIBUTED BY

HAL•LEONARD®

D1597121

Produced by Chas Chandler
Engineer: Eddie Kramer

Art Direction: Ed Thrasher
Cover Designed by David King
& Roger Law

Remastered by Eddie Kramer
& George Marino,
Sterling Sound, N.Y.
Remastering Supervision by
Janie Hendrix & John McDermott
for Experience Hendrix, L.L.C.
Booklet Design: Smay Vision

EXP

Announcer:	Good Evening, ladies and gentlemen. Welcome to Radio Station EXP. Tonight, we are featuring an interview with a very peculiar looking gentleman who goes by the name of Mr. Paul Corusoe, on the dodgy subject of are there or are there not flying saucers or . . . ahem. UFO's. Please Mr. Corusoe, please could you give your regarded opinion on this nonsense about spaceships and even space people.
Mr. Corusoe:	Thank you. As you all know, you just can't believe everything you see and hear, can you. Now, if you will excuse me, I must be on my way.
Announcer:	Bu . . . but, but . . . glub . . . I, I, don't believe it
Mr. Corusoe:	Pffffttt!! . . . Pop!! . . . Bang!! . . . Etc!!!?

UP FROM THE SKIES

I just want to talk to you. I won't do you no harm,
I just want to know about your different lives, on
    this here people farm.

I heard some of you got your families, living in
    cages tall & cold,
And some just stay there and dust away, past the
    age of old.
Is this true? Please let me talk to you.

I just want to know about, the rooms behind
    your minds,
Do I see a vacuum there, or am I going blind?
Or is it just remains from vibrations and echoes
    long ago,
Things like 'Love the World' and 'Let your fancy
    flow',
Is this true? Please let me talk to you. Let me
    talk to you.

I have lived here before, the days of ice,
And of course this is why I'm so concerned,
And I come back to find the stars misplaced
    and the smell of a world that has burned.

The smell of a world that has burned.

Well, maybee, maybe it's just a change of
    climate.
I can dig it, I can dig it baby, I just want to see.

So where do I purchase my ticket,
I would just like to have a ringside seat,
I want to know about the new Mother Earth,
I want to see and hear everything,
I want to see and hear everything,
I want to see and hear everything.
Aw, shucks,
If my daddy could see me now.

SPANISH CASTLE MAGIC

It's very far away,
It takes about half a day,
To get there, if we travel by my a . . . . . dragonfly

No, it's not in Spain,
But all the same,
You know,
It's a groovy name
And the wind's just right.

Hang on. My Darling,
Hang on if you want to go
You know it's a really groovy place
And it's just a little bit of Spanish Castle Magic.

The clouds are really low,
And they overflow,
With cotton candy
And battle grounds,
Red and brown.

But it's all in your mind,
Don't think your time,
On bad things,
Just float your little mind around.
Look out
Hang on, my Darling, Yeah
Hang on if you want to go
It puts everything else on the shelf
With just a little bit of Spanish Castle Magic
Just a little bit of daydream here and there.

Hang on, My Darling, Yeah
Hang on if you want to go
It puts everything else on the shelf
With just a little bit of Spanish Castle Magic
Just a little bit of daydream here and there.

WAIT UNTIL TOMORROW

Well, I'm standing here freezing, inside your
   golden garden,
Got my ladder leaned up against your wall.
Tonight's the night we planned to run away
   together,
Come on Dolly Mae, there's no time to stall.
But now you're telling me that ah . . .

I think we better wait till tomorrow
                              "
                        "
Got to make sure it's right,
So, until tomorrow, goodnight.

Oh, Dolly Mae, How can you hang me up this way,
On the phone you said you wanted to run off
   with me today
Now I'm standing here like some turned-down
   serenading fool,
Hearing strange words stutter from the mixed-up
   mind of you.
And you keep telling me that ah . . .

I think we better wait till tomorrow
                              "
                        "
Got to make sure it's right
So, until tomorrow, goodnight.
See if I can talk to this girl alone

Oh, Dolly Mae, girl, you must be insane,
So unsure of yourself leaning from your unsure
   window pane
Do I see a silhouette of somebody pointing
   something from a tree?
CLICK, BANG,
Oh, what a hang,
Your daddy just shot poor me
And I hear you say, as I fade away

We don't have to wait till tomorrow
                              "
                        "
It must not have been right, so forever,
   goodnight.
Do I have to wait, do I have to wait
Its a drag on my part
Don't have to wait, don't have to wait.

AIN'T NO TELLING

Well, there ain't no,
Ain't no
Ain't no telling, baby
When you will see me again, but I pray
It will be tomorrow.

Well, the sunrise
Sunrise
Is burning my eyes, baby
I must leave now, but I really hope
To see you tomorrow

Well my house is, oh, such a sad mile away,
The feeling there always hangs up my day
Oh, Cleopatra, She's driving me insane,
She's trying to put my body in her brain.
So just kiss me goodbye, just to ease the pain.
Ain't no
Ain't no
Ain't no telling baby
Ain't no telling babe
Ain't no telling baby when you're gonna see me,
    but I really hope
It will be tomorrow
You know what I'm talking 'bout.
Ain't no telling
Sorry, but I must leave now

LITTLE WING

Well, she's walking through the clouds,
With a circus mind that's running wild,
Butterflies and Zebras,
And Moonbeams and fairy tales.
That's all she ever thinks about.
Riding with the wind.

When I'm sad, she comes to me,
With a thousand smiles she gives to me free.
It's alright, she says it's alright,
Take anything you want from me,
Anything.
Fly on little wing.

IF 6 WAS 9

Yeah, sing the song, Bro'

If the sun refuse to shine,
I don't mind, I don't mind,
If the mountains fell in the sea,
Let it be, it ain't me.
Alright, 'cos I got my own world to look through,
And I ain't gonna copy you.

Now if 6 turned out to be 9,
I don't mind, I don't mind,
Alright, if all the hippies cut off all their hair,
I don't care, I don't care.
Dig, 'cos I got my own world to live through
And I ain't gonna copy you.

White collared conservative flashing down the
    street,

Pointing their plastic finger at me.
They're hoping soon my kind will drop and die,
But I'm gonna wave my freak flag high, high.
Wave on, wave on
Fall mountains, just don't fall on me
Go ahead on Mr. Business man, you can't
    dress like me.
Sing on Brother, play on drummer.

YOU GOT ME FLOATIN'

You got me floatin' round and round,
Always up, you never let me down
The amazing thing, you turn me on naturally,
And I kiss you when I please.

You got me floatin' round and round,
You got me floatin' never down
You got me floatin' naturally
You got me floatin' float to please

You got me floatin' across and through
You make me float right on up to you
There's only one thing I need to really get me
    there,
Is to hear you laugh without a care.

You got me floatin' round and round,
You got me floatin' never down
You got me floatin' naturally
You got me floatin' float to please

You got me floatin' round and round
You got me floatin' never down
You got me floatin' naturally
You got me floatin' float to please

Now your Daddy's cool, and your Mamma's no
    fool,
They both know I'm heads over heels for you,
And when the day melts down into a sleepy red
    glow,
That's when my desires start to show.

You got me floatin' round and round
You got me floatin' never down
You got me floatin' naturally
You got me floatin' float to please.

CASTLES MADE OF SAND

Down the street you can hear her scream
  "you're a disgrace"
As she slams the door in his drunken face,
And now he stands outside and all the
  neighbours start to gossip and drool.

He cries "Oh girl, you must be mad,
What happened to the sweet love you and me
  had?"
Against the door he leans and starts a scene,
And his tears fall and burn the garden green.

And so castles made of sand, fall in the sea,
  eventually.

A little Indian brave who before he was ten,
  played war games in
the woods with his Indian friends, and he built
  a dream that when he
grew up, he would be a fearless warrior Indian
  Chief.

Many moons passed and more the dream grew
  strong, until tomorrow
He would sing his first war song,
And fight his first battle, but something went
  wrong,
Surprise attack killed him in his sleep that night

And so castles made of sand, melts into the
  sea eventually.

There was a young girl, whose heart was a frown,
Because she was crippled for life, and couldn't
  speak a sound
And she wished and prayed she would stop living,
  so she decided to die.
She drew her wheel chair to the edge of the
  shore, and to her legs she smiled

"You won't hurt me no more."
But then a sight she'd never seen made her
  JUMP AND SAY
"Look, a golden winged ship is passing my way"
And it really didn't have to stop . . . it just kept
  on going.
And so castles made of sand slips into the sea,
Eventually

Jimi Hendrix had barely put the finishing touches on *Are You Experienced*, the group's remarkable 1967 debut album, before he began recording new songs for what would ultimately become *Axis: Bold As Love*. Less than nine months had passed since Chas Chandler had brought Jimi Hendrix to London in September 1966. With Chandler installed as his manager and producer, the two formed the Jimi Hendrix Experience with drummer Mitch Mitchell and bassist Noel Redding. On the strength of early singles like "Hey Joe," "Purple Haze," and "The Wind Cries Mary," the Experience had conquered England and Europe. The group's stunning performance at the June 1967 Monterey Pop Festival and the subsequent release of *Are You Experienced* won over American fans and clearly illustrated the magnitude of the trio's capabilities. While touring and other commitments would delay further *Axis: Bold As Love* recording sessions for the new album until October 1967, the unquenchable creative fire burning within the belly of the Experience would soon produce another gem. Avidly gathered and explored by the public, the thirteen majestic songs of *Axis: Bold As Love* proved that Jimi Hendrix was no one album wonder.

Not satisfied with mining the same vein that had yielded the motherlode of *Are You Experienced*, the Experience kicked off their sophomore effort with a novelty step into the science fiction milieu that Jimi loved. "EXP" featured a faux radio announcer, played by drummer Mitch Mitchell, interviewing Jimi posing as Paul Carusoe, an expert on alien life. The track launched thirty-eight minutes of some of the most brilliant rock to be etched in vinyl the entire year. It contains a phenomenal group of songs. "Spanish Castle Magic," "You Got Me Floatin'," the title track, "Bold As Love," and the now standard, "Little Wing". Few would attempt to argue the album's timelessness. The range of emotions and styles expressed throughout *Axis* equals those found on *Are You Experienced*, but there is a different quality about them. The time between the initial sessions for the "Hey Joe" single to the final touches on "She's So Fine" for *Axis* was only a year. The Experience had spent the time well. From the full out rockers to softer poetic outings, *Axis: Bold As Love* was chock full of well crafted pop songs.

Chas Chandler's contribution in that vein should not be overlooked. Chas had learned a great deal about pop music structure as the bassist for the Animals, one of the most successful groups of the British invasion. His knowledge was in full display on *Are You*

...we are the life-giving water...
...taking for granted...they quietly un...
once-happy Torquoise Armys lay opposite...
BUT wondering why the fight is on...Just ask the
But their all bold as love...

Red...sunday...s
....dash

So confident, he c̶a̶i̶
Trophies of war and
Ribbons of

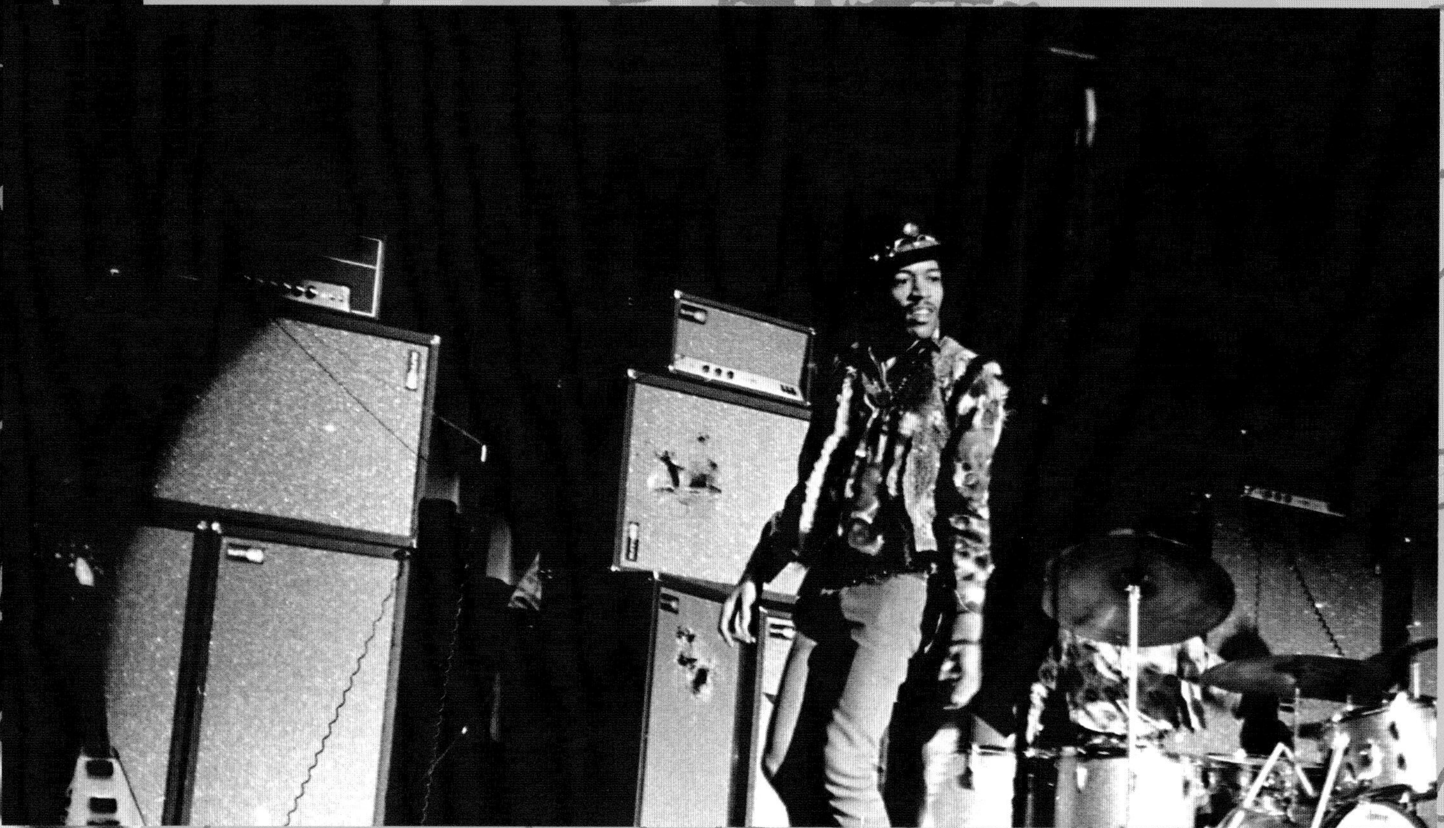

B.
rc
EL
FA...
...like me...Its

Experienced, where he was clearly in charge. It is to his credit that he recognized Jimi's remarkable growth as a musician and composer. By the *Axis* sessions he and Jimi were equal partners in creative matters. His influence reined in some of Jimi's more extravagant impulses that later reemerged with new discipline on *Electric Ladyland*. The longest song on Axis, "If 6 Was 9" runs 5:32. Of the other eleven songs, only "One Rainy Wish" and "Bold As Love" exceeded the three minute AM top-forty radio barrier of the day. Unquestionably, Chas had carried his message well.

Just as important in the history of the Jimi Hendrix Experience was how the band reacted to their incredible initial successes. Many bands have found early success a distraction and a recipe for dissolution. The *Axis* days for Jimi and the Experience, on the other hand, were some of the happiest in the short tempestuous life of the group. That joy translated easily to disc and was clearly apparent throughout the sessions for the album. The trio created a union that, on the surface, might have seemed unlikely, but one that used its disparate influences to form a union of three with a single soul.

Mitch Mitchell brought his love of jazz, and Philly Joe Jones in particular, to the table, and his adroit stickmanship and machine gun fills reflects that interest throughout *Axis*. For example, Mitch's breaks on "Wait Until Tomorrow" come right out of

the hard bop book. His brush work (at Noel's suggestion) on "Up From The Skies" would be just as at home in a smoky jazz piece as on this funky science fiction rocker.

Noel Redding was a converted guitar player and brought a guitarist's sensibilities and deftness to the bass. His style pushed Jimi and Mitch into a tight union normally reserved for the tightest of bassist and drummer combinations. This coalition was a key element on *Axis*. Listen to the delicate interplay within "One Rainy Wish" founded on that well-established rhythmic rapport. With "She's So Fine," Noel's own composition, the bassist assumed the lead vocal, leading Jimi and Mitch through this charged rocker. From start to finish, Noel's offerings were an integral part of this fine album.

Jimi's own passions involved the great bluesmen such as Buddy Guy, soulsters like Curtis Mayfield and jazzmen like Wes Montgomery. Those influences are apparent all through the *Axis: Bold As Love* album sessions. The soft rhythmic flow of "Little Wing" bears Curtis' imprint and in Jimi's opening rhythmic line to "Wait Until Tomorrow" we hear him tipping his hat to the R&B and Soul riffs he learned in his days on the chitlin' circuit. Ironically, though Jimi heard the intricate line clearly enough in his head, he had difficulty reproducing it in the studio, according the engineer on the sessions, Eddie Kramer. He obviously got it right eventually.

Kramer was another important part of the *Axis* effort. He and Jimi had, by this time, forged an important kinship. With Chandler's full confidence and support, Kramer was astute enough to recognize Jimi's understanding of mixing and catered to Hendrix's suggestions. *Axis: Bold As Love* was his second album with the Experience and he had developed an uncanny ability to grasp what Jimi had in his mind and was willing to work doggedly to achieve it on tape. Jimi, especially when discussing subtleties of sound, would often describe what he wanted to hear in terms of colors. Eddie was able to develop a palette that Jimi could paint with. And when Jimi said he dreamed of having his guitar sound like he was playing it underwater, Kramer, along with fellow Olympic studio engineer George Chkiantz, developed the technique of phasing to make that dream come true. The coda at the end of the title track illustrates a remarkable use of the technique.

Axis was not an album which could be easily translated into live performance, nor was it intended to be. In the first place, the songs had not been road tested like those on *Are You Experienced*. They were built from the ground up in the studio and the various effects that were added to the album (including a glockenspiel on "Little Wing") were not intended to be part of the group's thrilling live gigs. In fact only "Spanish Castle Magic" and sometimes "Little Wing" were ever regularly performed by the group. In Jimi's mind the two areas were completely separate. On stage, Jimi's message was entirely singular and he made the most of his opportunity to connect with his audience. The recording studio required a different focus, a different way of communicating through his music.

Axis: Bold As Love almost became a failure to communicate. After deciding on the thirteen tracks which would make the final cut, the firm of Hendrix, Kramer and Chandler began the laborious task of creating a final mix. After finishing the job in the early hours of Halloween, 1967, Hendrix and Chas Chandler took the master tapes home to the apartment they shared. Somehow, the unthinkable happened. Jimi misplaced the mixes for the album's first side. Since the tapes had been removed before any safeties were made, their loss was truly a disaster. The mixes had been made from four-track originals and their creation had been a performance unto itself. Needless to say no one was happy with the task that faced them, remixing the half inch tapes and trying to recreate what they had finished once already. With the lucrative Christmas season fast approaching, and the album already scheduled for release, the mixing had to be accomplished in one night.

"If 6 Was 9" was the one track they just couldn't seem to get right. Each attempt had the team scratching their heads knowing that the sound wasn't right. Despite a number of attempts, neither Chandler, Hendrix, nor Kramer were sure as to how they had achieved the earlier mix. Exasperated, they dispatched Noel in a cab to find a seven-and-a-half inch, three inch reel containing a rough mix from June that the bassist had at his apartment. The tape turned out to be badly wrinkled and needed to be ironed in order to get it through the studio machine. The mix was finally accomplished though, and beautifully so. From then on, the high praise Chandler and Kramer enjoyed for their labor has always brought on a sardonic smile. "If you only knew," Chandler would often laugh.

For the listener, the extra effort was well worth it. With *Axis: Bold As Love* Jimi and company had created a magnificent and groundbreaking album that has stood the test of time. It remains not only a faithful document of its era, but it is just as relevant today as it was nearly thirty years ago. Since its initial release, *Axis: Bold As Love* has remained both a critical and a fan favorite. Though Jimi has been gone longer than he lived, we are fortunate to live in a time in which recordings keep his genius at our call. *Axis* is definitive proof both of that genius and the magnitude of our loss.

Jym Fahey

BOOKLET PHOTOGRAPHY: Baron Wolman (pg10,19,22-23), Wilson Lindsey/Star File (pg11),
Eddie Kramer (pg12), Leni Sinclair (pg13), Linda McCartney/Star File (pg15,18,21),
Bruce Fleming (pg16-17)

INSIDE INLAY PHOTOGRAPH: Petra Niemeier/Star File (pg4/left),

For more information about Jimi Hendrix please write:
    Experience Hendrix
    PO Box 4130
    Seattle, Washington 98104

Or visit us on the World Wide Web at: Experience Hendrix Interactive
http://www.jimi-hendrix.com

If you would like to purchase Authentic Jimi Hendrix merchandise CALL: 1-888-EXP-JIMI

EXP

Words and Music by Jimi Hendrix

Announcer: *Good evening ladies and gentlemen.*
Welcome to radio station EXP.
Tonight we are featuring an interview with a very peculiar looking gentleman
who goes by the name of Mr. Paul Corusoe, on the dodgy subject of: Are there
or are there not flying saucers or...ahem, UFO's?

Um...Please, Mr. Corusoe, could you give us your regarded opinion on this
nonsense about spaceships, and even space people?

Mr. Corusoe: *Thank you.*
As you all know, you just can't believe everything you see and hear. Can you?
Now, if you'll excuse me, I must be on my way.

Announcer: *Bu...but, but...glub...I, I don't believe it.*

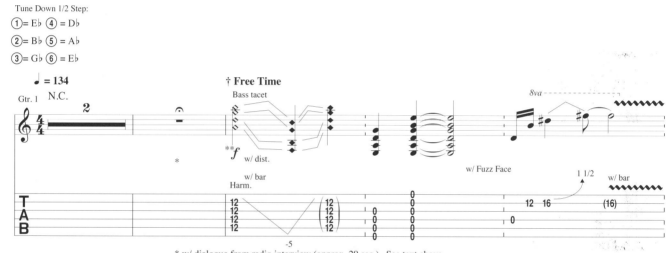

* w/ dialogue from radio interview (approx. 29 sec.). See text above.

** Audio is faded in and out, panning right to left for duration of track.

† No time signature.

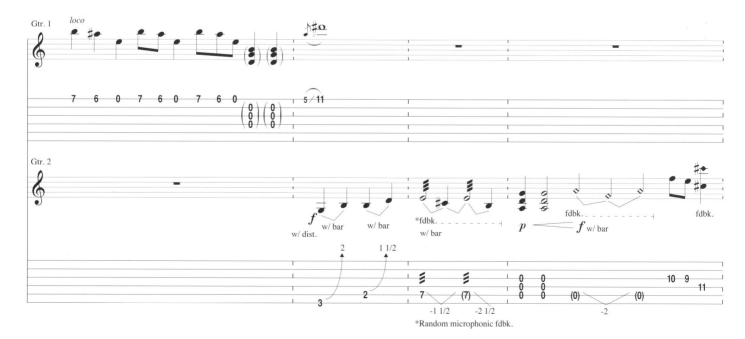

*Random microphonic fdbk.

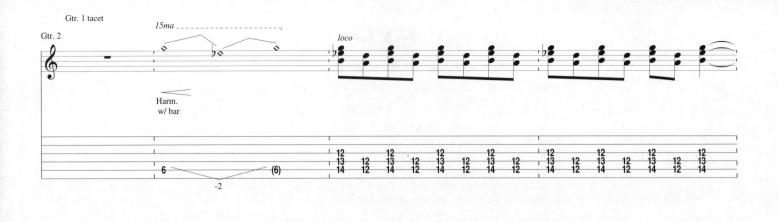

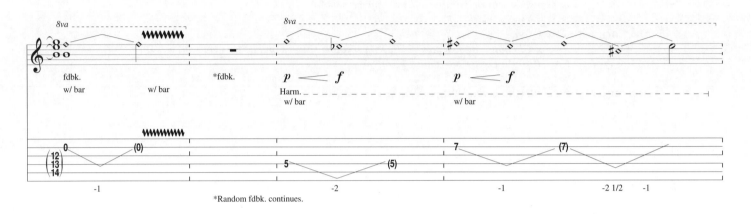

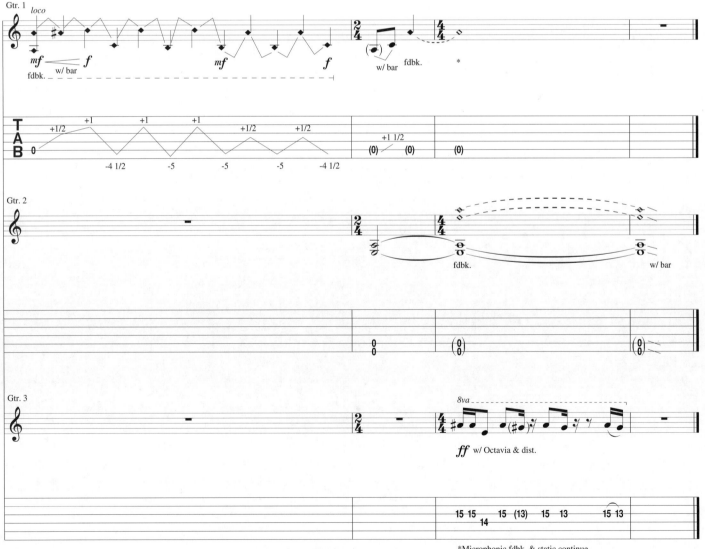

Up from the Skies

Words and Music by Jimi Hendrix

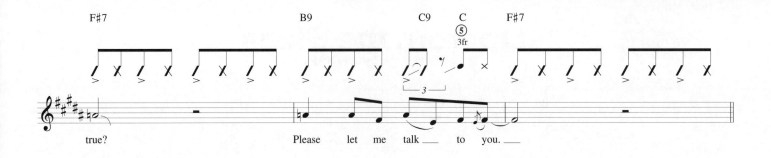

true?   Please   let me talk   to you.

Verse

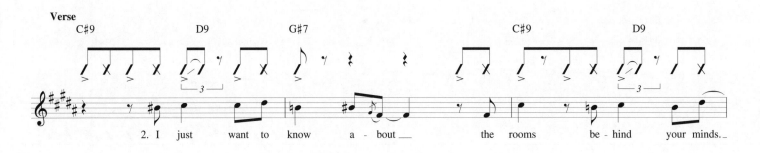

2. I   just   want to   know   a - bout   the   rooms   be - hind your minds.

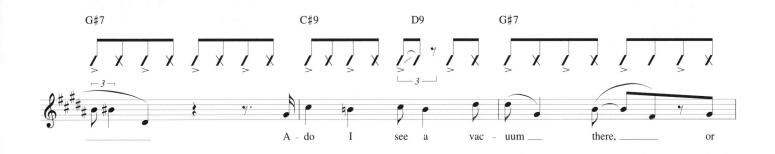

           A - do   I   see   a   vac - uum   there,   or

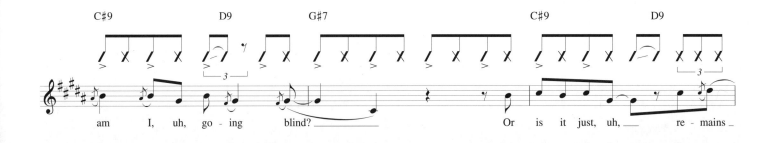

am   I, uh, go - ing   blind?   Or   is it just, uh,   re - mains

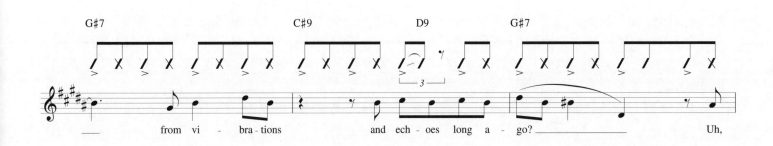

        from vi - bra - tions   and ech - oes long a - go?   Uh,

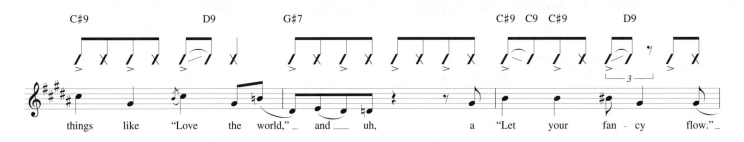

things   like   "Love   the   world,"   and   uh,   a   "Let   your   fan - cy   flow."

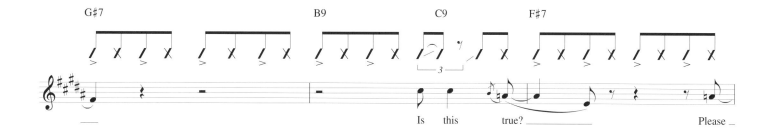

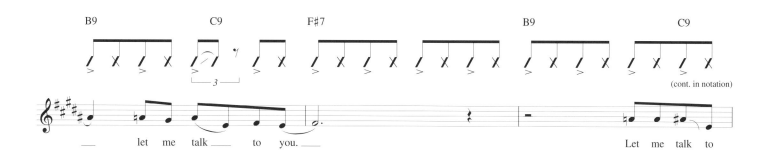

* Bridge

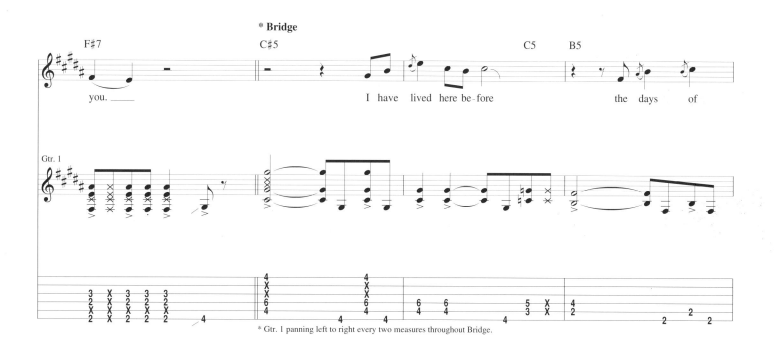

* Gtr. 1 panning left to right every two measures throughout Bridge.

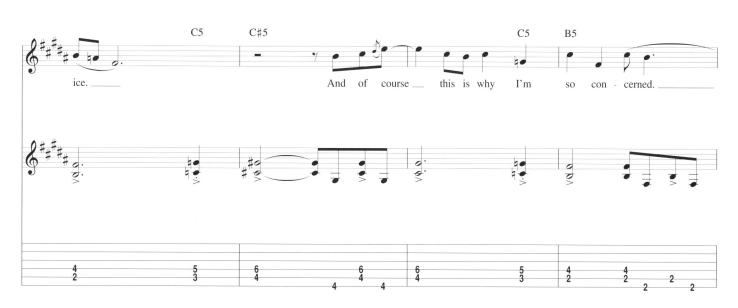

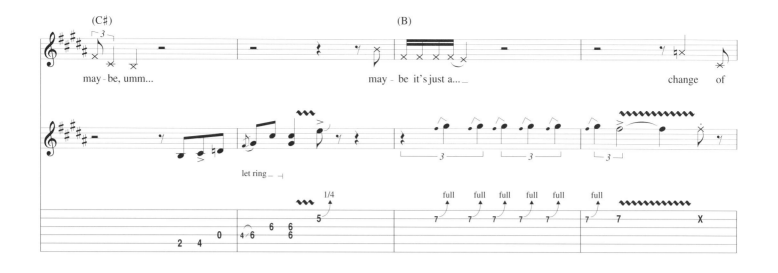

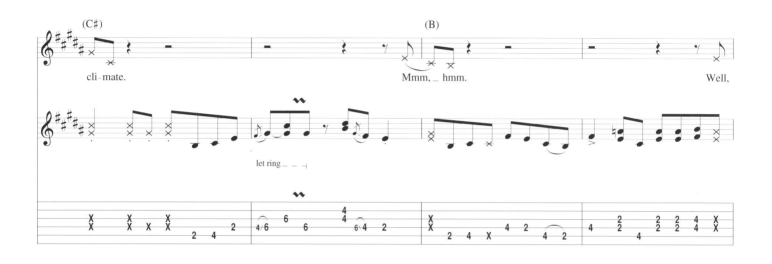

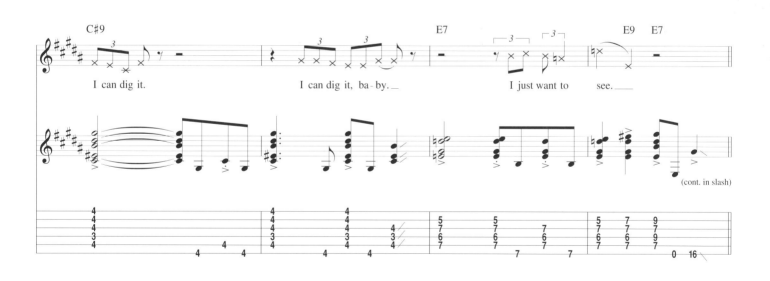

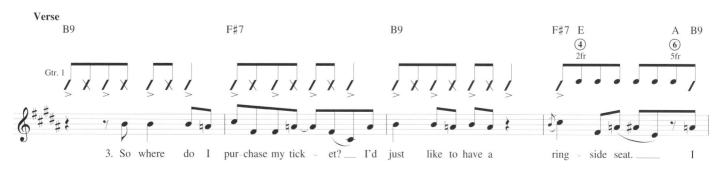

want to know a-bout the new Moth-er Earth, _ I want to hear and see _____ ev-'ry-thing. _____ I

(cont. in notation)

want to hear and see ev-'ry-thing. _____ I want to hear and see _____

* Guitar Solo

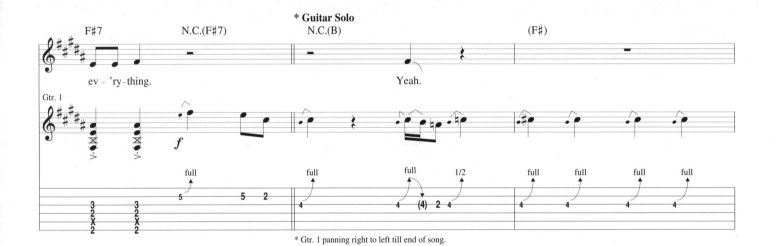

ev-'ry-thing. Yeah.

* Gtr. 1 panning right to left till end of song.

even

Begin Slow Fade

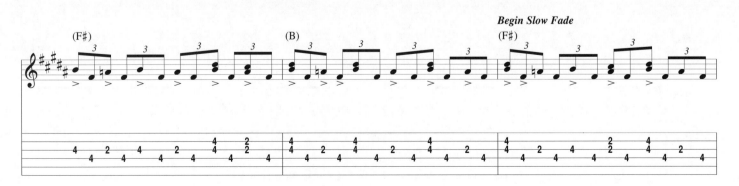

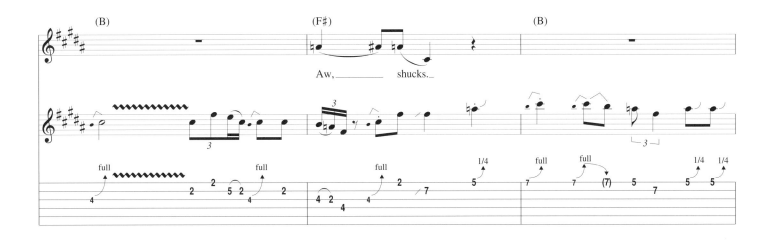

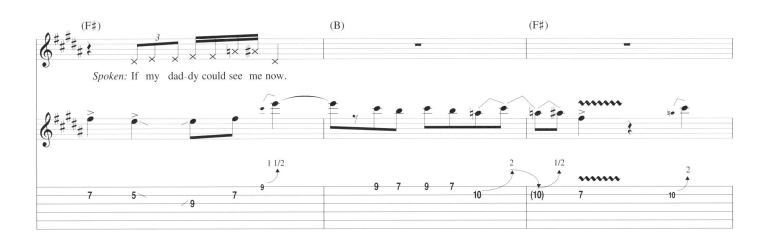

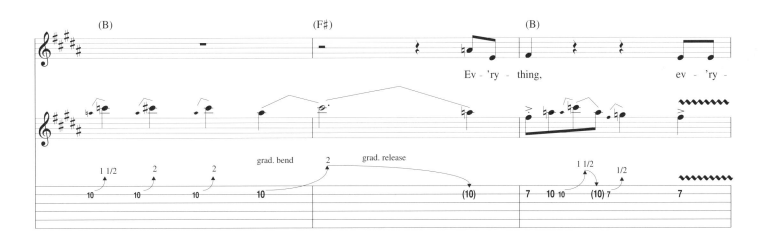

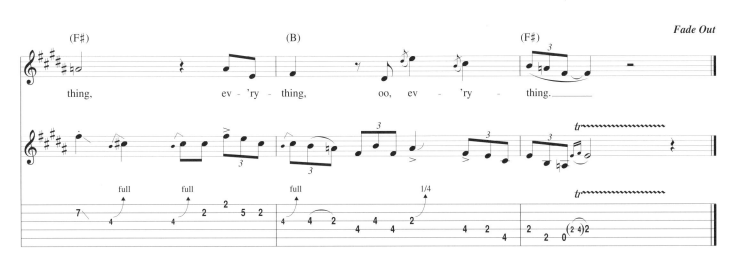

Spanish Castle Magic

Words and Music by Jimi Hendrix

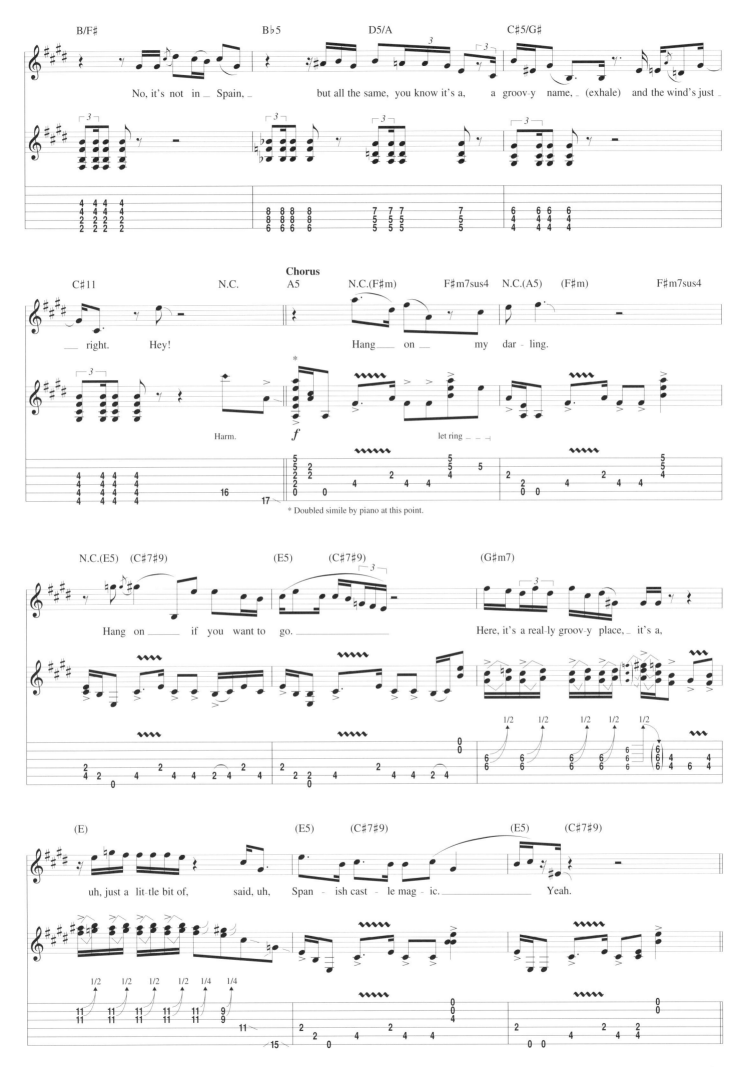

* Doubled simile by piano at this point.

* Played behind the beat.

Wait until Tomorrow

Words and Music by Jimi Hendrix

Tune Down 1/2 Step:
① = E♭ ④ = D♭
② = B♭ ⑤ = A♭
③ = G♭ ⑥ = E♭

Intro
Moderate Rock ♩ = 118

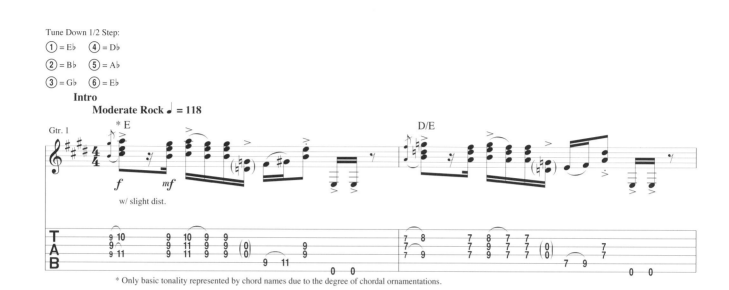

* Only basic tonality represented by chord names due to the degree of chordal ornamentations.

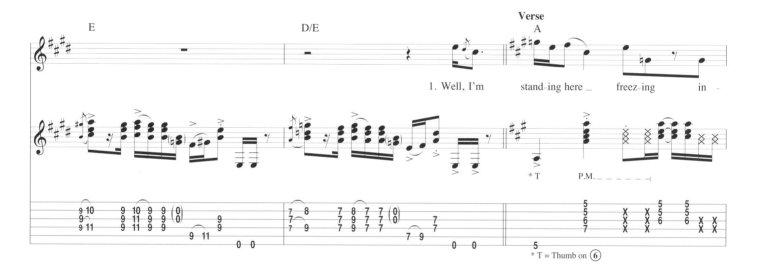

* T = Thumb on ⑥

Ain't No Telling

Words and Music by Jimi Hendrix

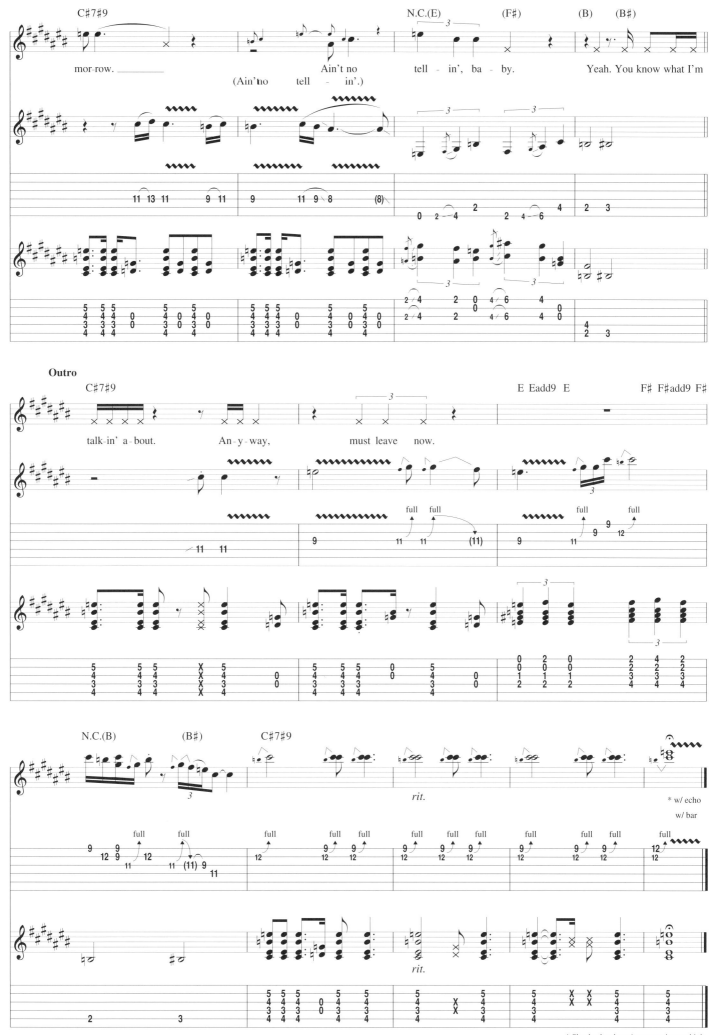

* Slap back echo w/ regeneration set high.

Little Wing

Words and Music by Jimi Hendrix

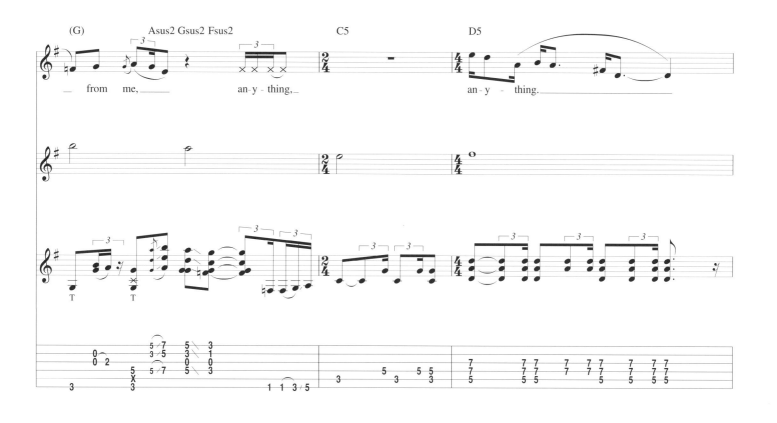

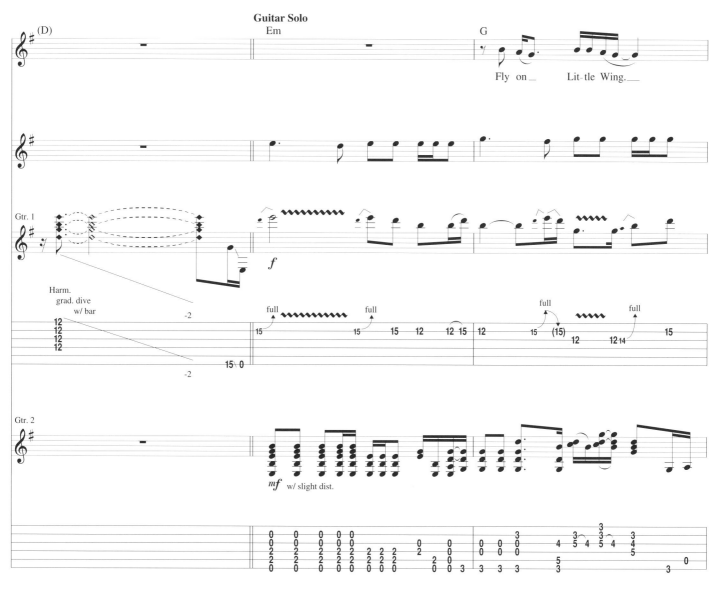

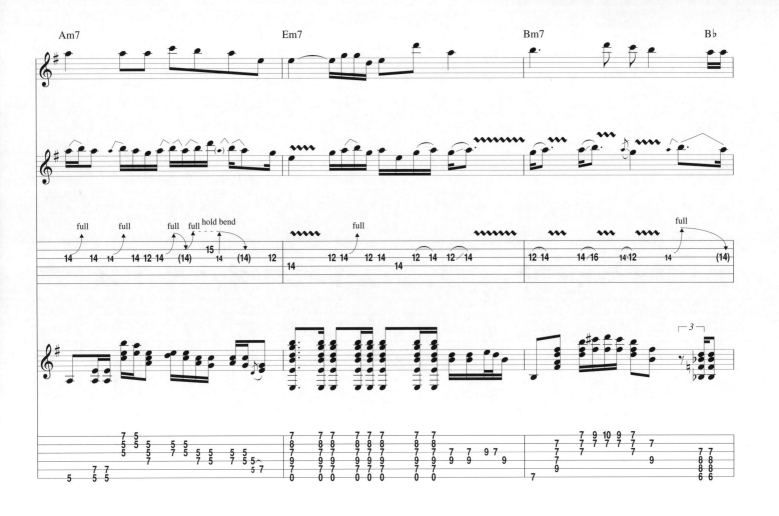

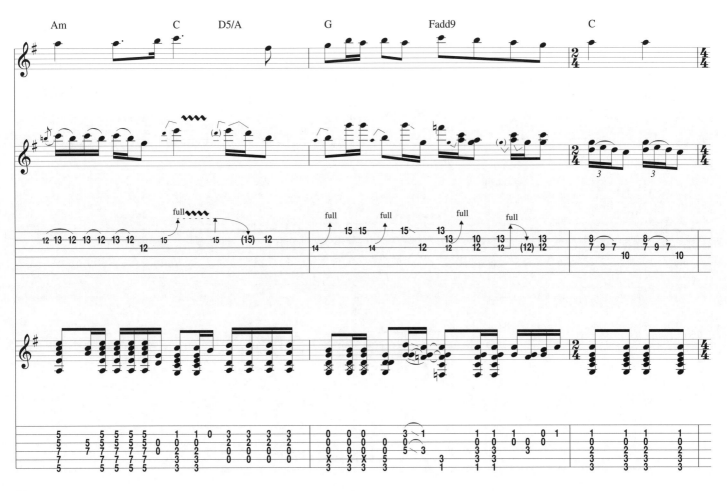

If Six Was Nine

Words and Music by Jimi Hendrix

you can't dress like   me.   Yeah. _

End Riff A

* **Drum Solo**
Gtr. 1: w/ Riff A, 1 1/5 times   **12**

* w/ voc. ad Lib (next 12 meas.)

Verse

Spoken: 4. Don't no-bod-y know what I'm talk-in' a-bout?   I've got my own

Gtr. 1

mp

life to live.   I'm the one that's gon-na have to die   when it's   time for me to die,

so let me live my life   the way I want to.

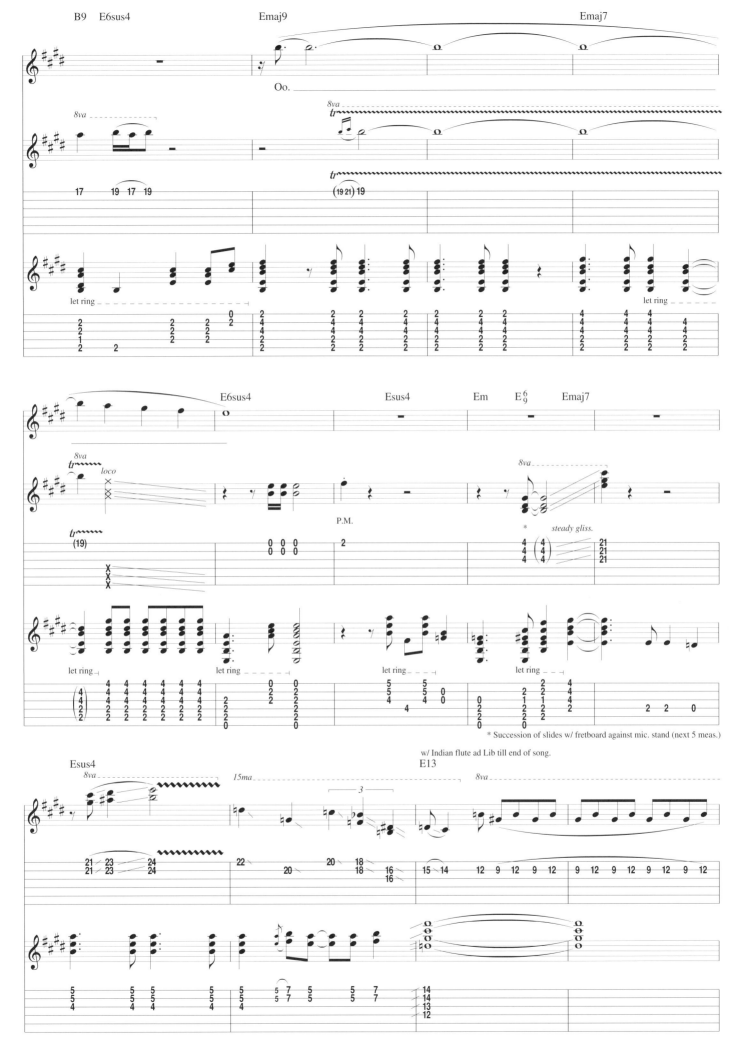

* Succession of slides w/ fretboard against mic. stand (next 5 meas.)

w/ Indian flute ad Lib till end of song.

You Got Me Floatin'

Words and Music by Jimi Hendrix

* Backwards guitar.

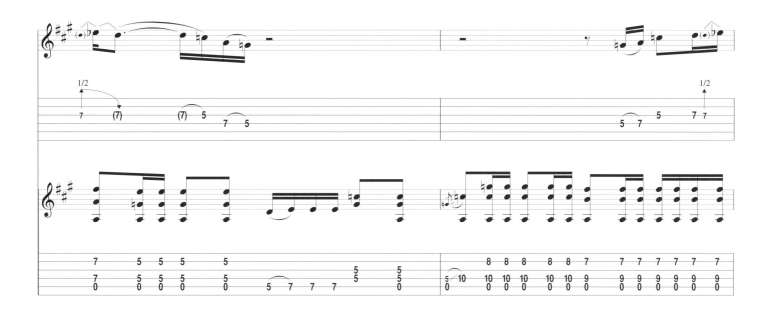

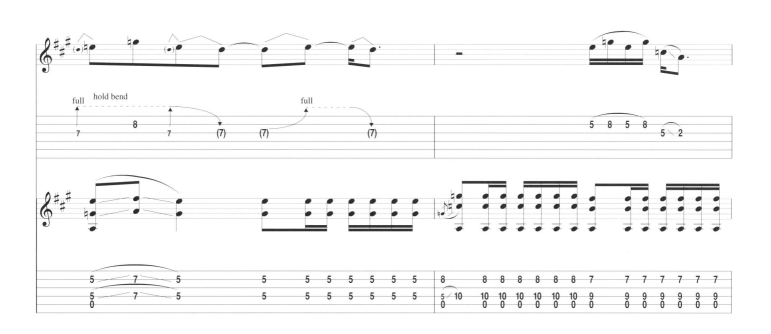

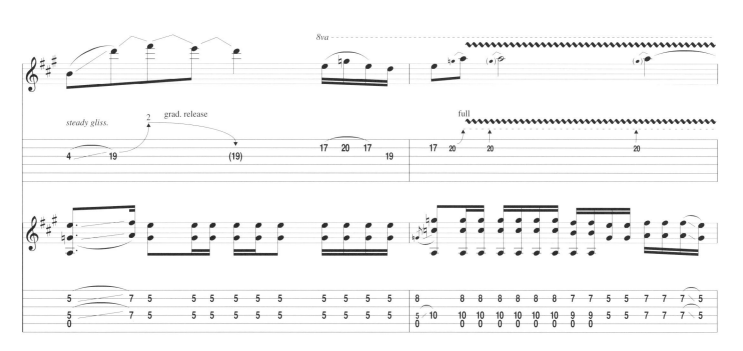

Chorus

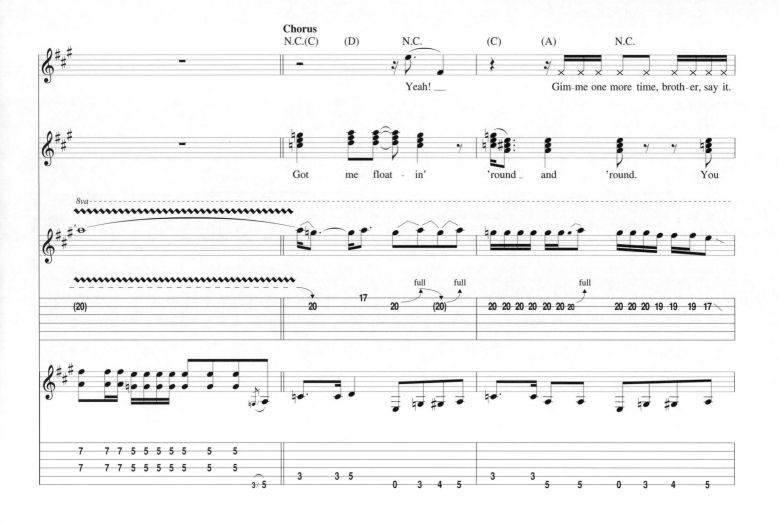

80

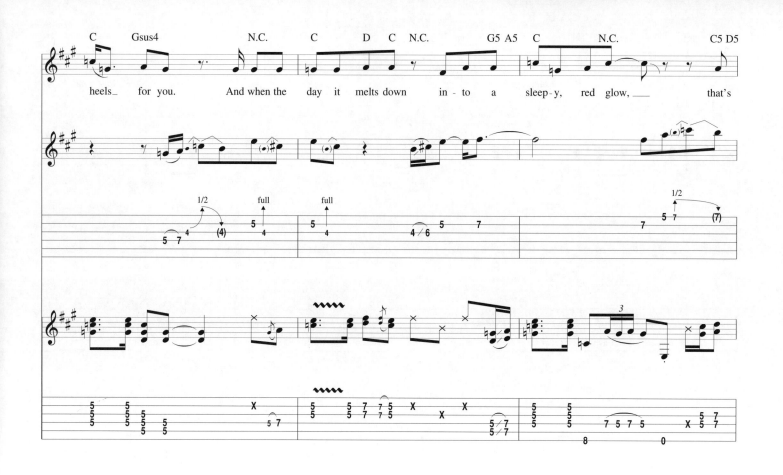

heels___ for you. And when the day it melts down in - to a sleep - y, red glow, ___ that's

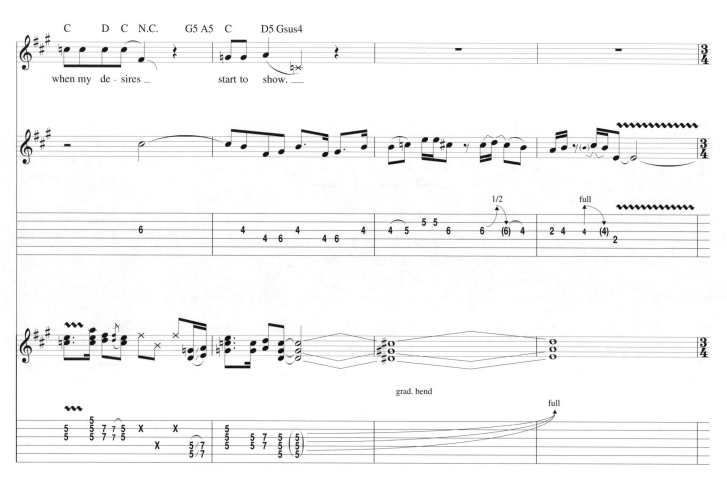

when my de - sires ___ start to show. ___

grad. bend

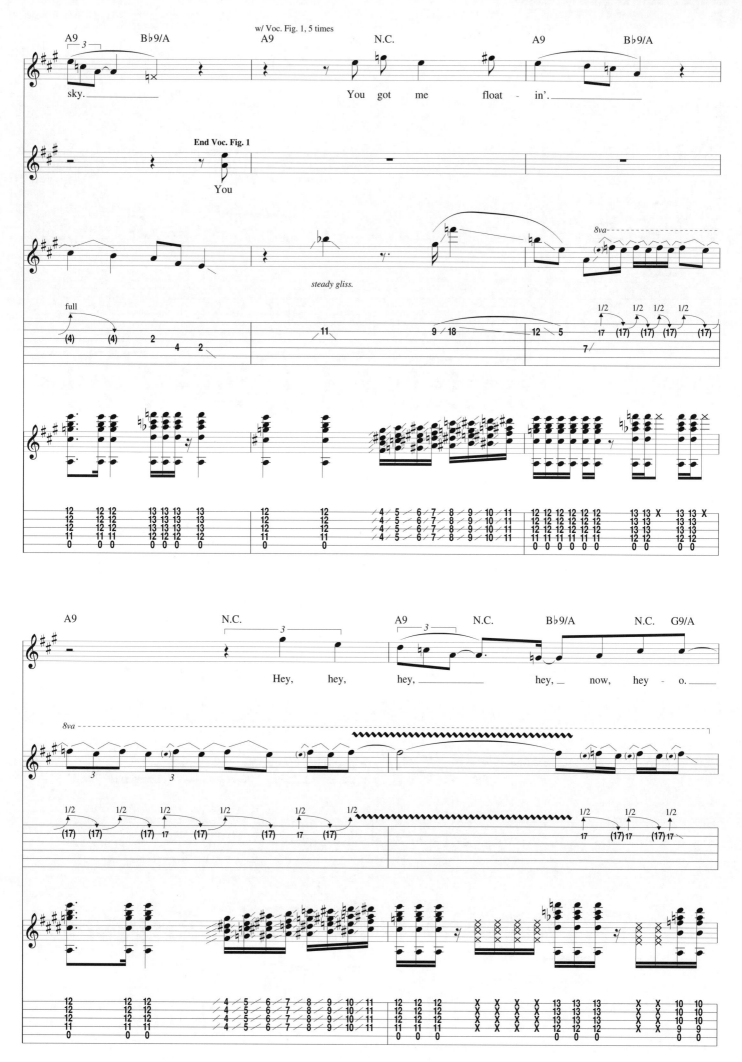

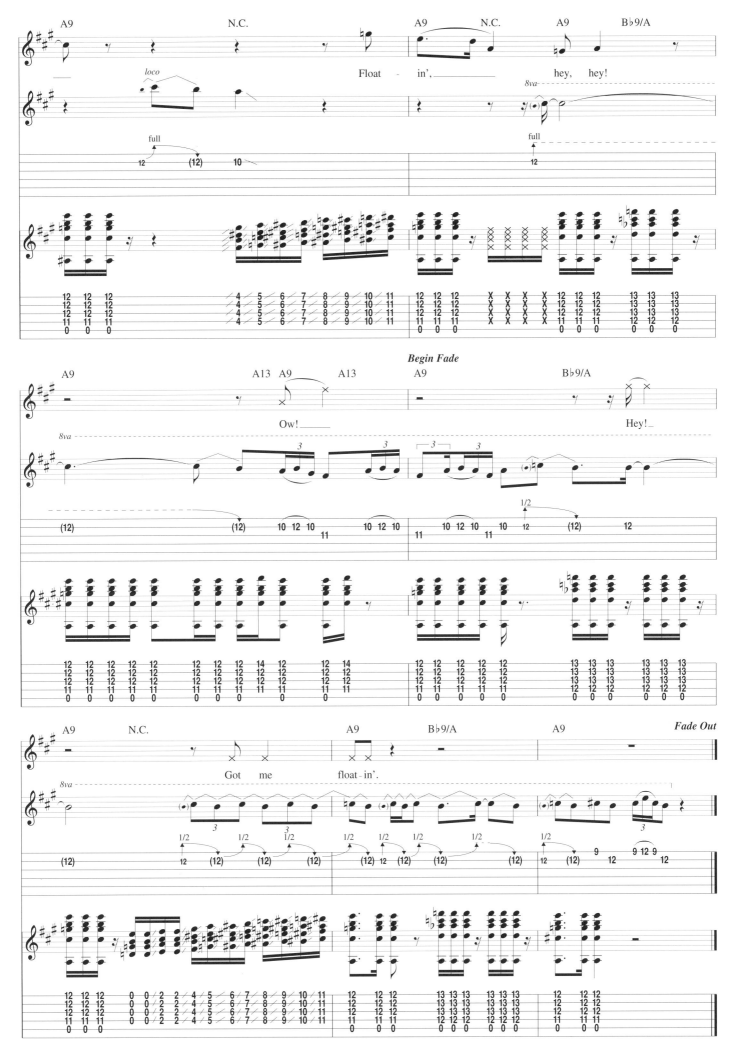

Castles Made of Sand

Words and Music by Jimi Hendrix

Tune Down 1/2 Step:
①= Eb ④= Db
②= Bb ⑤= Ab
③= Gb ⑥= Eb

Intro
Freely ♩ = 126

1. Down the street you can hear her scream, "You're a dis - grace," as she

** Backwards guitar. *T=Thumb on ⑥

* Vibrato G intermittently "bumps into" C note, 3rd str., 5th fret.

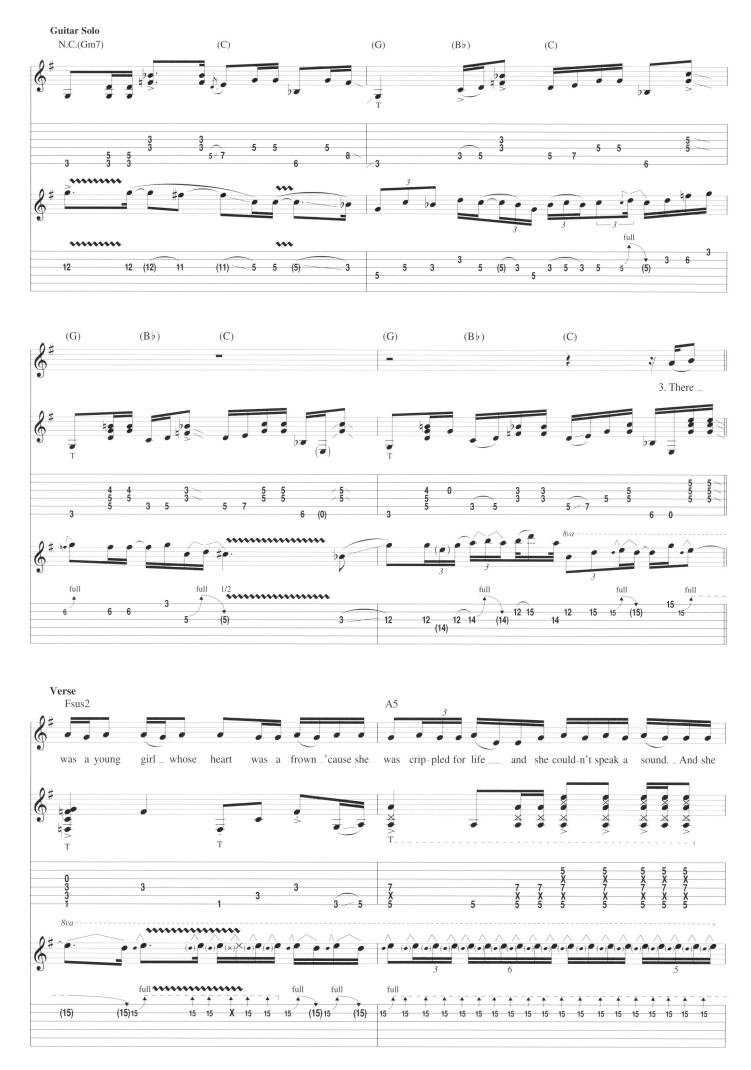

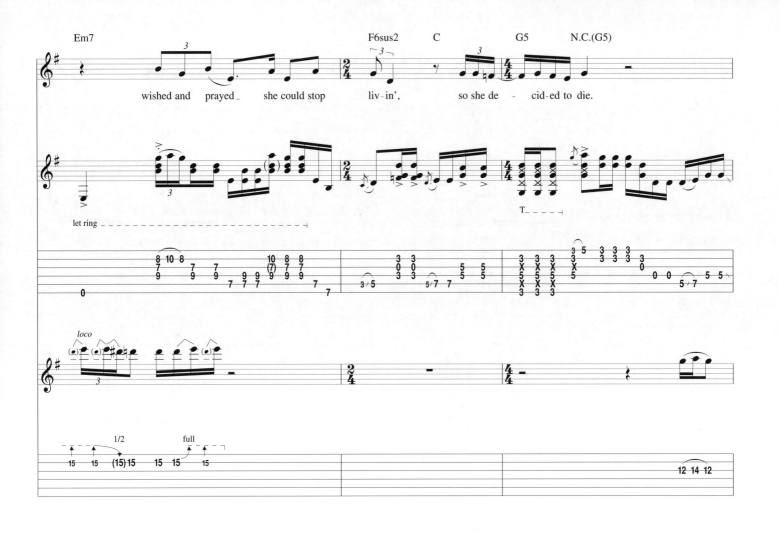

wished and   prayed__   she could stop   liv-in',   so she de - cid-ed to die.

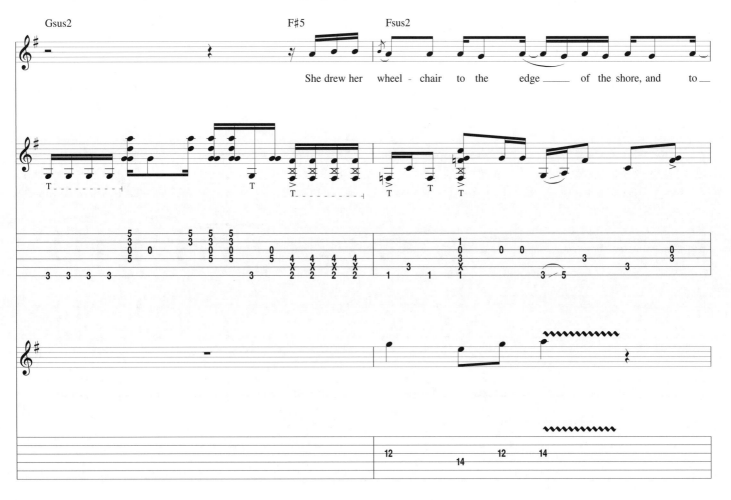

She drew her   wheel - chair   to the   edge _____ of the shore, and   to __

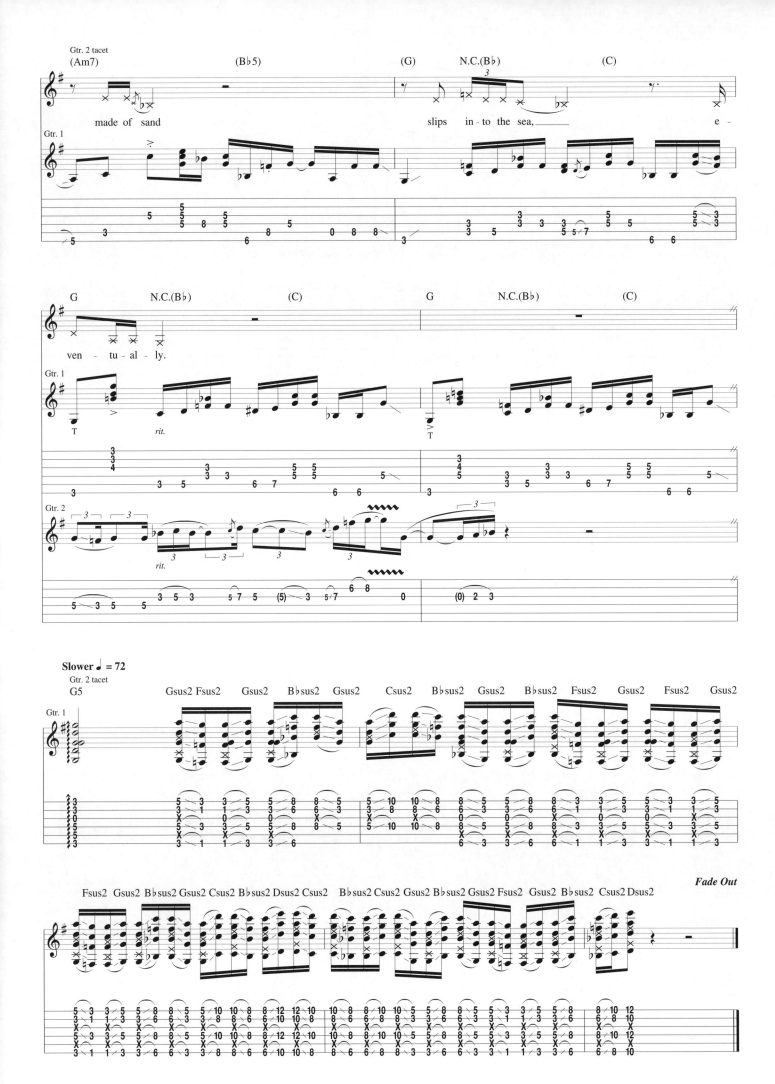

She's So Fine

Words and Music by Noel Redding

*Key signature denotes A Mixolydian.

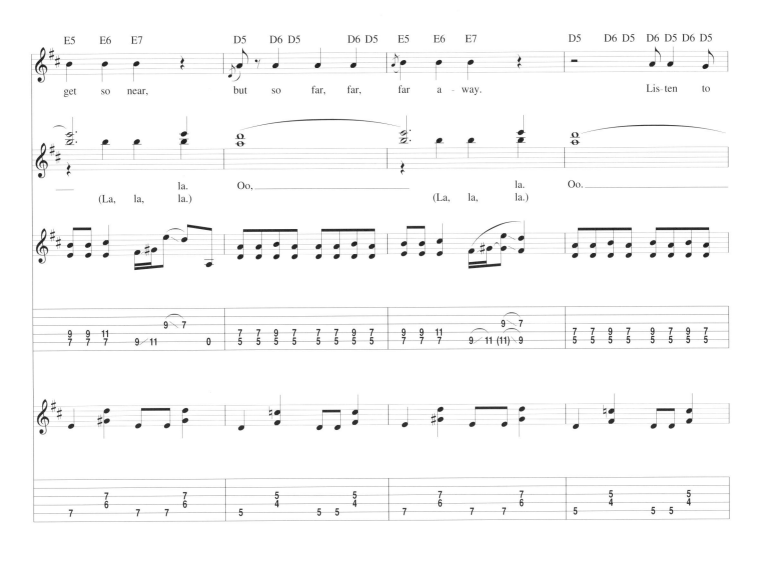

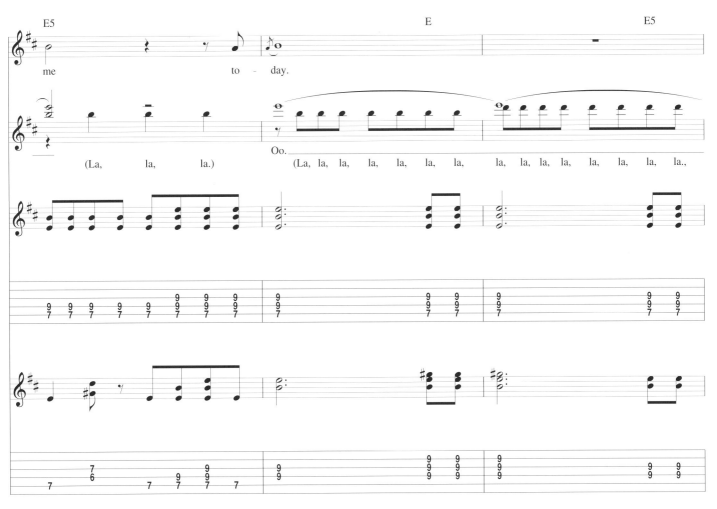

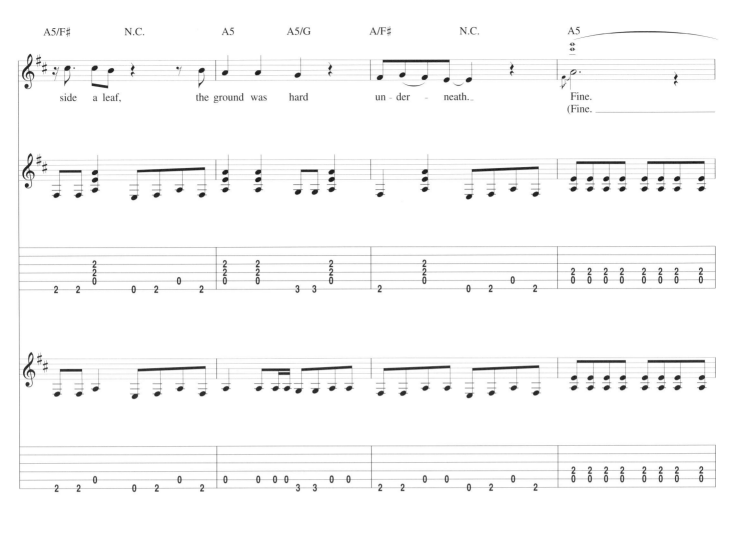

side a leaf, the ground was hard un - der - neath.___ Fine.
(Fine.___

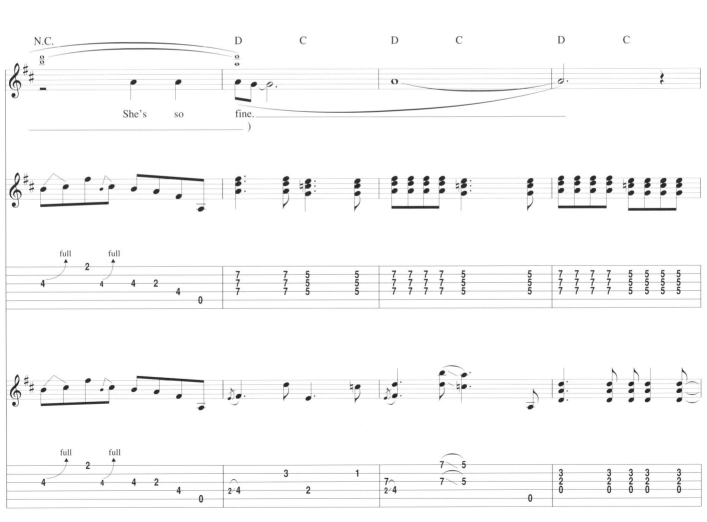

She's so fine.___)

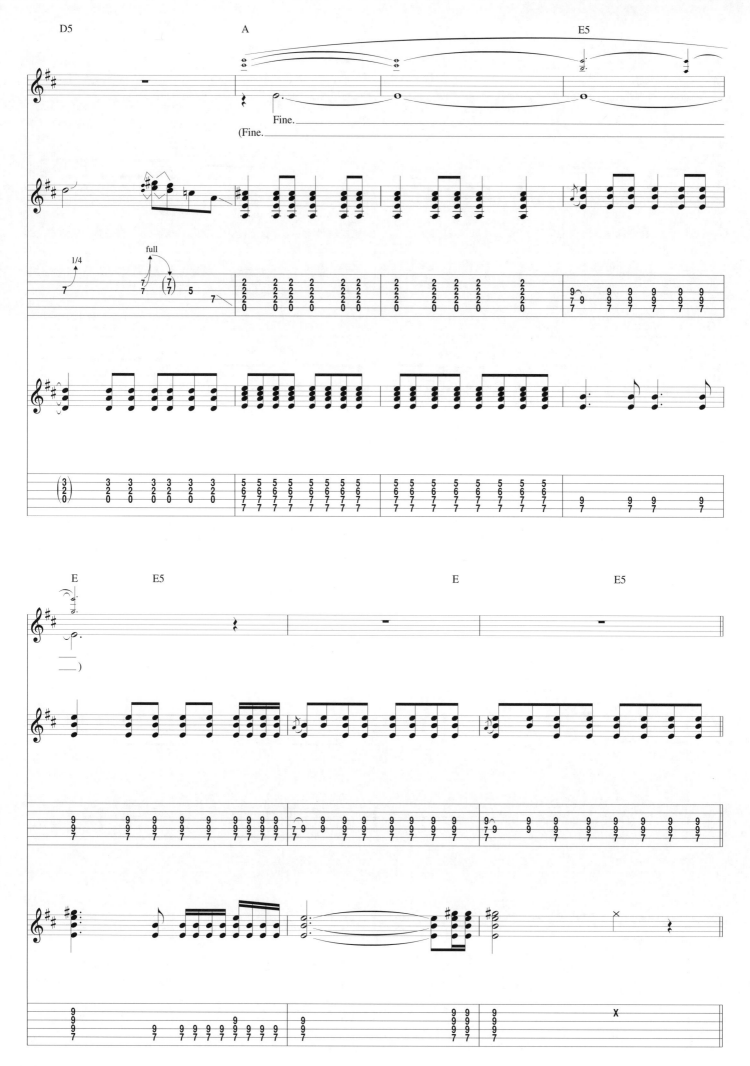

One Rainy Wish

Words and Music by Jimi Hendrix

*Chord symbols reflect basic implied tonality.

Chorus

*I have nev-er laid eyes on you, a like a be-fore this time-less day. Ah, but you walked and ya once

*Double tracked vocal.

Guitar Solo

Gold - en __ rose, __   gold - en __ rose, __   gold - en __ rose. __

Outro

Oo. __

Oo. __

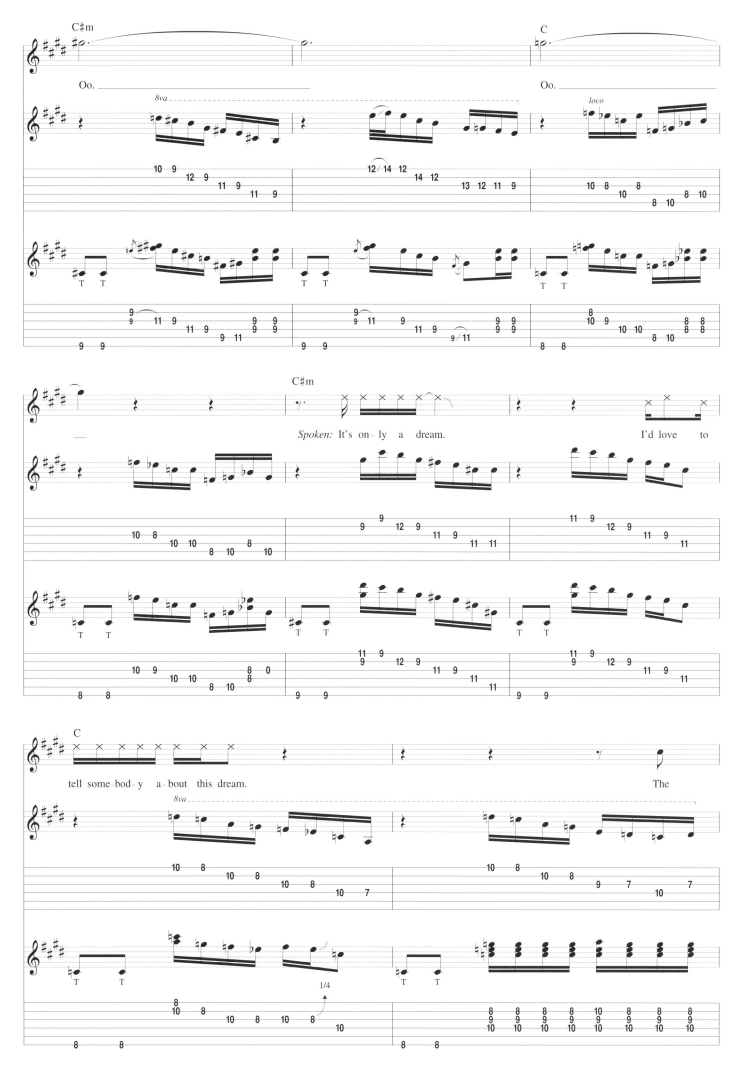

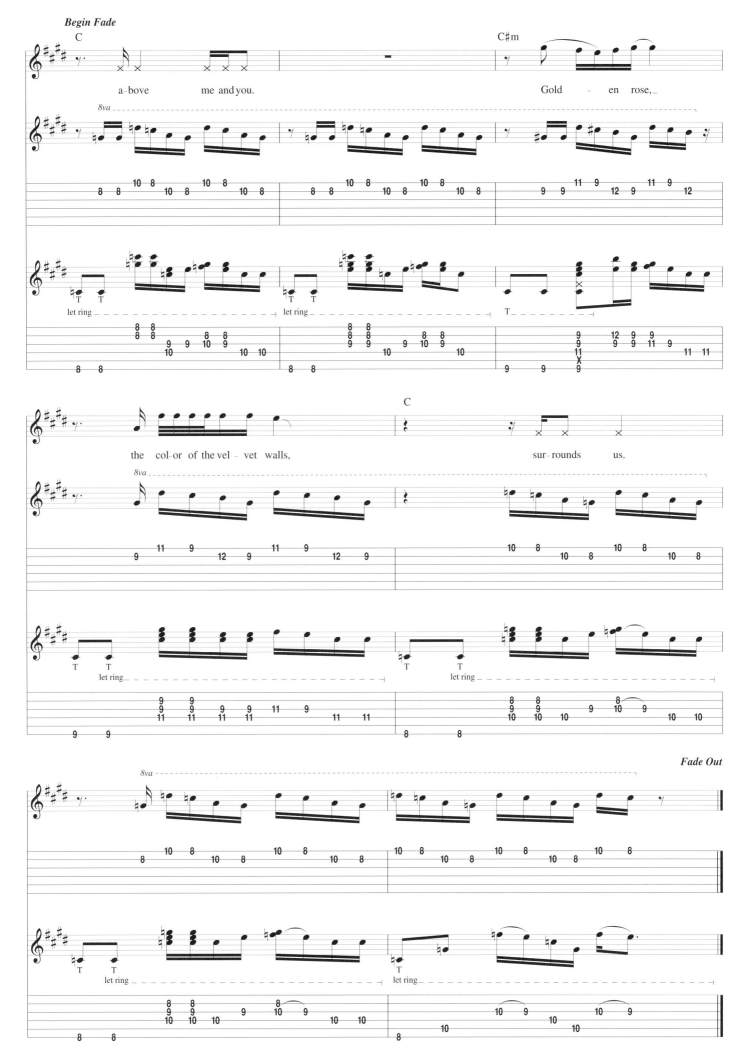

Little Miss Lover

Words and Music by Jimi Hendrix

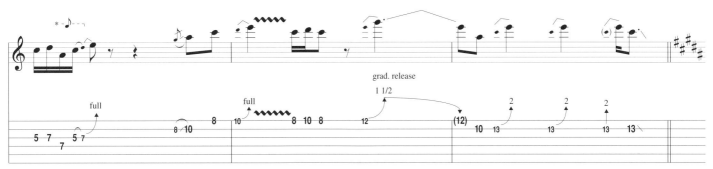

* Played behind the beat.

Chorus

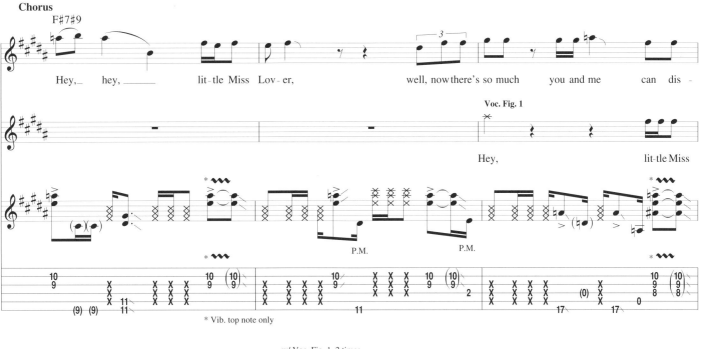

* Vib. top note only

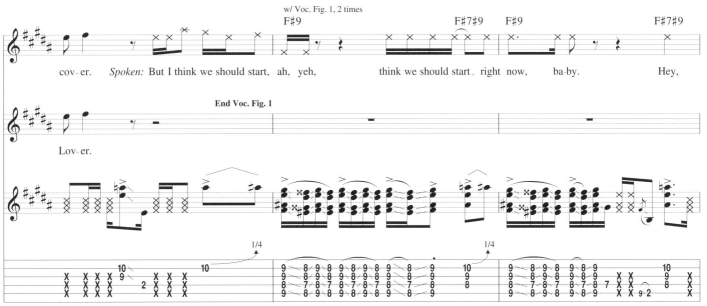

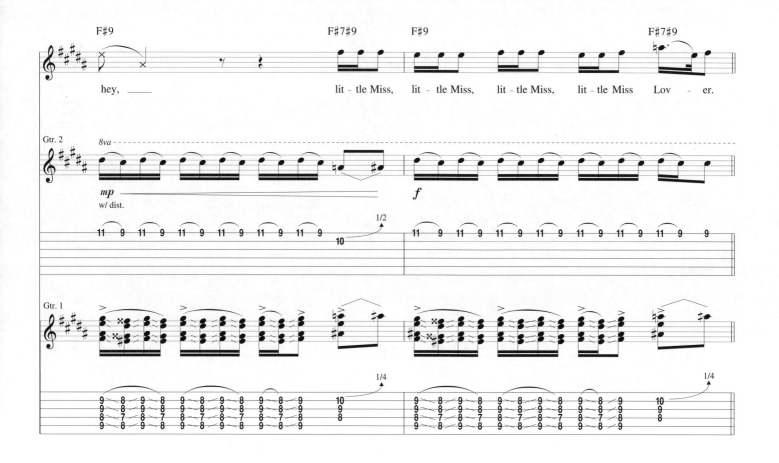

Outro

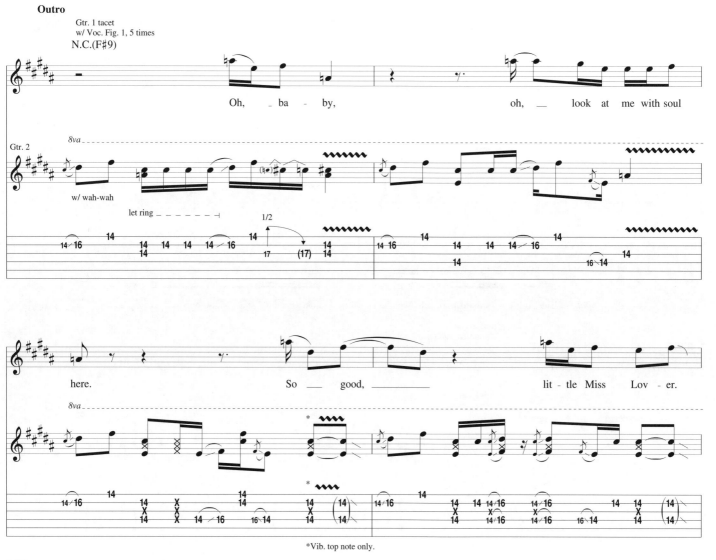

*Vib. top note only.

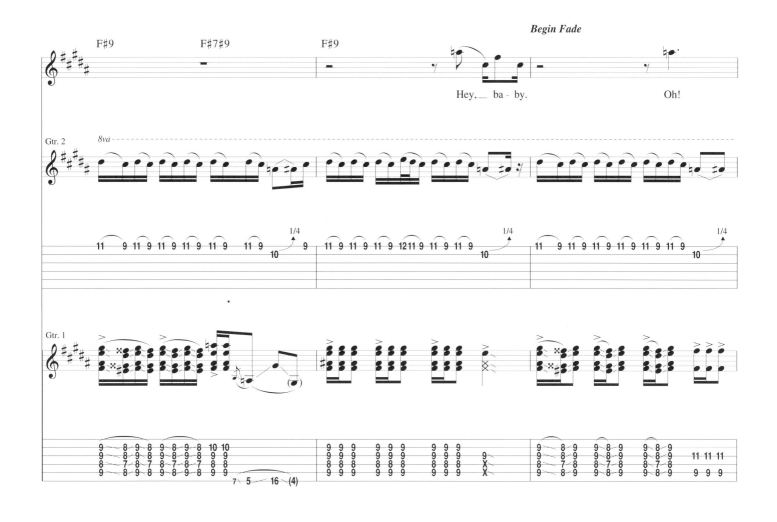

Hey, ___ ba - by.   Oh!

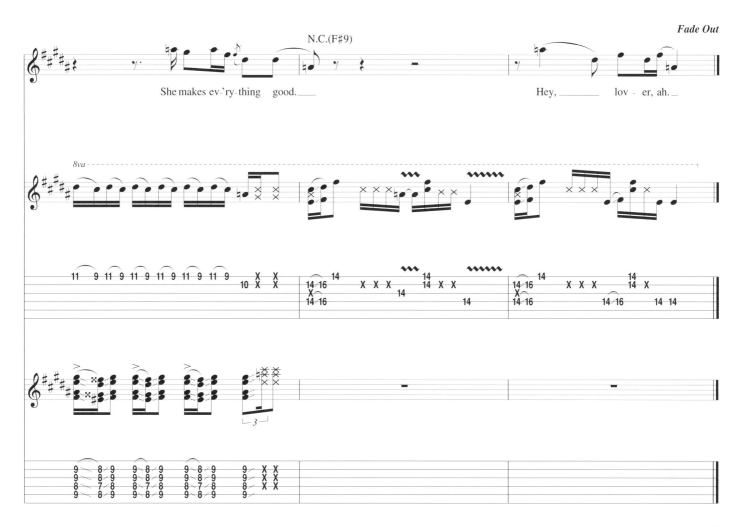

She makes ev-'ry-thing good. ___   Hey, ___ lov - er, ah. ___

Bold as Love

Words and Music by Jimi Hendrix

Once hap - py tur-quoise arm - ies lay op-po-site, read - y, but won-der why the fight is on. ____

Chorus

But they're all ____ bold ____ as love.

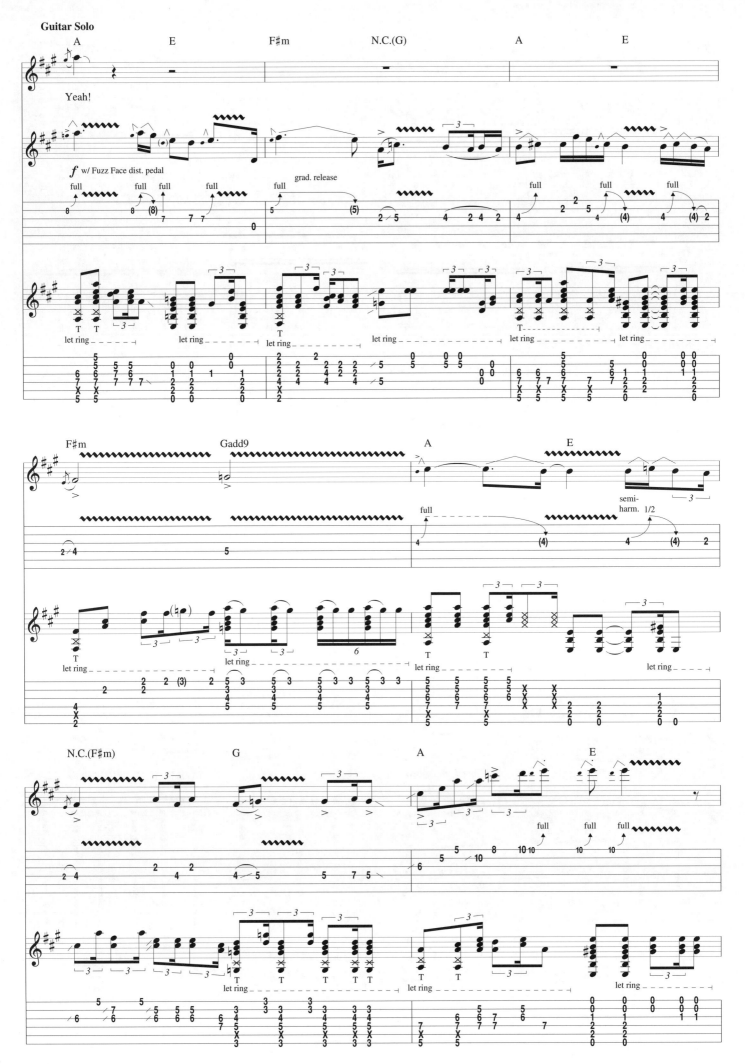

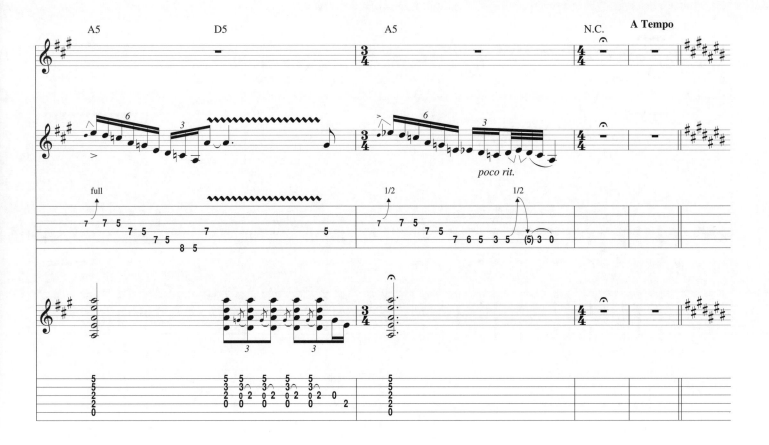

Outro Solo

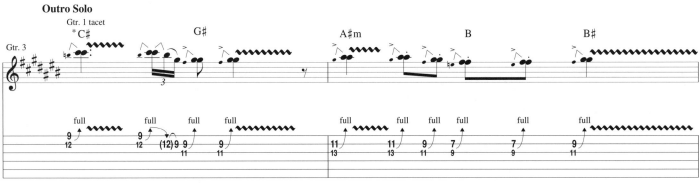

* Chords played to Mellotron (early kybd. sampler that utilized tapes vs. electronics) for remainder of tune.

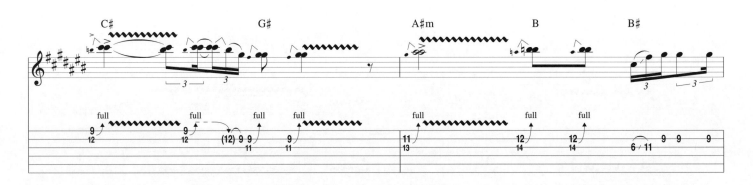

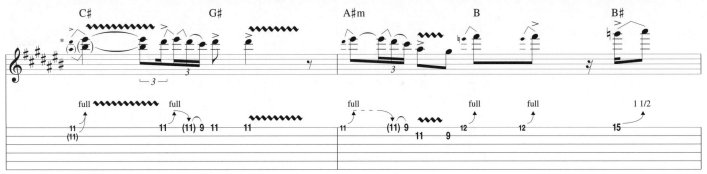

* 2nd string sounds unintentionally.

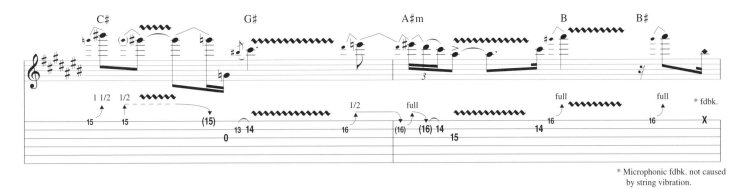

* Microphonic fdbk. not caused
  by string vibration.

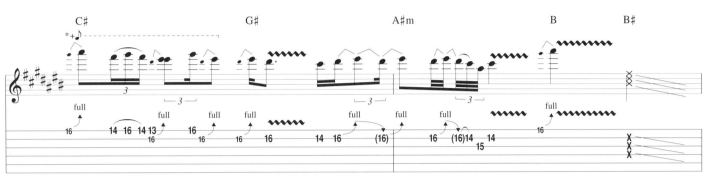

* Played ahead of the beat.

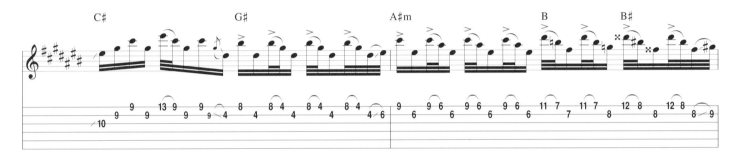

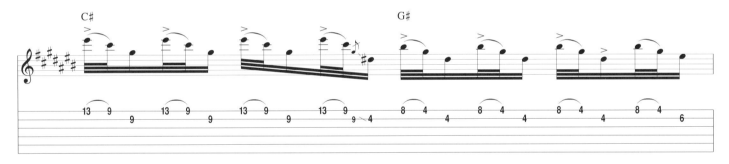

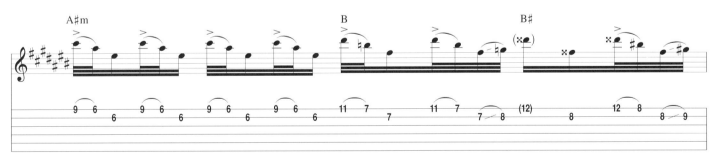

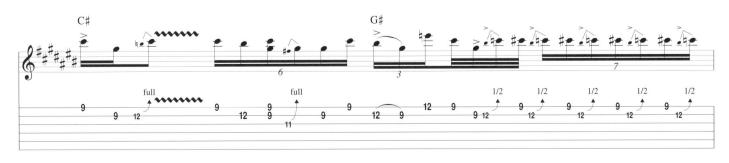

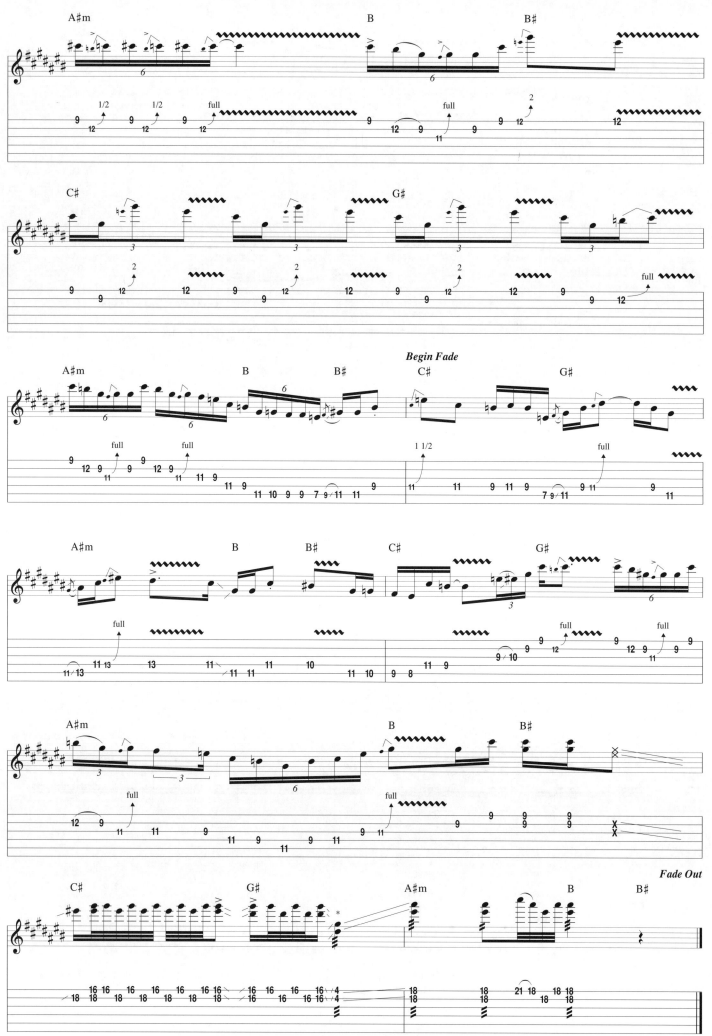

* Trem. pick and slide up simultaneously.

Guitar Notation Legend

Guitar Music can be notated three different ways: on a *musical staff*, in *tablature*, and in *rhythm slashes*.

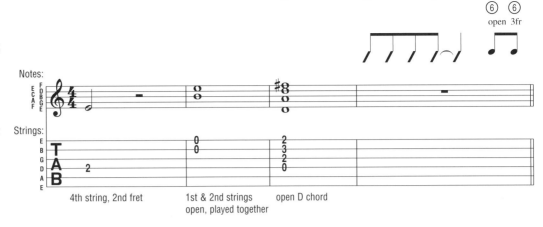

RHYTHM SLASHES are written above the staff. Strum chords in the rhythm indicated. Use the chord diagrams found at the top of the first page of the transcription for the appropriate chord voicings. Round noteheads indicate single notes.

THE MUSICAL STAFF shows pitches and rhythms and is divided by bar lines into measures. Pitches are named after the first seven letters of the alphabet.

TABLATURE graphically represents the guitar fingerboard. Each horizontal line represents a a string, and each number represents a fret.

Notes:

Strings:

4th string, 2nd fret

1st & 2nd strings open, played together

open D chord

Definitions for Special Guitar Notation

HALF-STEP BEND: Strike the note and bend up 1/2 step.

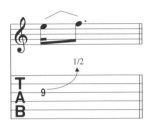

WHOLE-STEP BEND: Strike the note and bend up one step.

GRACE NOTE BEND: Strike the note and bend up as indicated. The first note does not take up any time.

SLIGHT (MICROTONE) BEND: Strike the note and bend up 1/4 step.

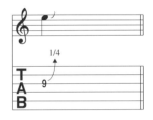

BEND AND RELEASE: Strike the note and bend up as indicated, then release back to the original note. Only the first note is struck.

PRE-BEND: Bend the note as indicated, then strike it.

PRE-BEND AND RELEASE: Bend the note as indicated. Strike it and release the bend back to the original note.

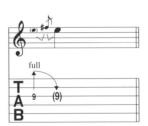

UNISON BEND: Strike the two notes simultaneously and bend the lower note up to the pitch of the higher.

VIBRATO: The string is vibrated by rapidly bending and releasing the note with the fretting hand.

WIDE VIBRATO: The pitch is varied to a greater degree by vibrating with the fretting hand.

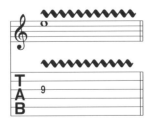

HAMMER-ON: Strike the first (lower) note with one finger, then sound the higher note (on the same string) with another finger by fretting it without picking.

PULL-OFF: Place both fingers on the notes to be sounded. Strike the first note and without picking, pull the finger off to sound the second (lower) note.

LEGATO SLIDE: Strike the first note and then slide the same fret-hand finger up or down to the second note. The second note is not struck.

SHIFT SLIDE: Same as legato slide, except the second note is struck.

TRILL: Very rapidly alternate between the notes indicated by continuously hammering on and pulling off.

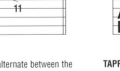

TAPPING: Hammer ("tap") the fret indicated with the pick-hand index or middle finger and pull off to the note fretted by the fret hand.

NATURAL HARMONIC: Strike the note while the fret-hand lightly touches the string directly over the fret indicated.

PINCH HARMONIC: The note is fretted normally and a harmonic is produced by adding the edge of the thumb or the tip of the index finger of the pick hand to the normal pick attack.

HARP HARMONIC: The note is fretted normally and a harmonic is produced by gently resting pick hand's index finger directly above the indicated fret (in parentheses) while the pick hand's thumb or pick assists by plucking the appropriate string.

PICK SCRAPE: The edge of the pick is rubbed down (or up) the string, producing a scratchy sound.

MUFFLED STRINGS: A percussive sound is produced by laying the fret hand across the string(s) without depressing, and striking them with the pick hand.

PALM MUTING: The note is partially muted by the pick hand lightly touching the string(s) just before the bridge.

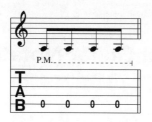

RAKE: Drag the pick across the strings indicated with a single motion.

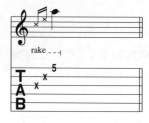

TREMOLO PICKING: The note is picked as rapidly and continuously as possible.

ARPEGGIATE: Play the notes of the chord indicated by quickly rolling them from bottom to top.

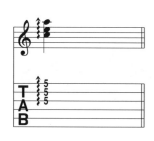

VIBRATO BAR DIVE AND RETURN: The pitch of the note or chord is dropped a specified number of steps (in rhythm) then returned to the original pitch.

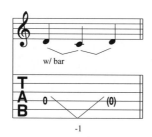

VIBRATO BAR SCOOP: Depress the bar just before striking the note, then quickly release the bar.

VIBRATO BAR DIP: Strike the note and then immediately drop a specified number of steps, then release back to the original pitch.

Additional Musical Definitions

  (accent) • Accentuate note (play it louder)

  (accent) • Accentuate note with great intensity

(staccato) • Play the note short

⊓ • Downstroke

∨ • Upstroke

D.S. al Coda • Go back to the sign (𝄋), then play until the measure marked "*To Coda*," then skip to the section labelled "*Coda*."

D.S. al Fine • Go back to the beginning of the song and play until the measure marked "*Fine*" (end).

Rhy. Fig. • Label used to recall a recurring accompaniment pattern (usually chordal).

Riff • Label used to recall composed, melodic lines (usually single notes) which recur.

Fill • Label used to identify a brief melodic figure which is to be inserted into the arrangement.

Rhy. Fill • A chordal version of a Fill.

tacet • Instrument is silent (drops out).

 • Repeat measures between signs.

 • When a repeated section has different endings, play the first ending only the first time and the second ending only the second time.

NOTE: Tablature numbers in parentheses mean:
1. The note is being sustained over a system (note in standard notation is tied), or
2. The note is sustained, but a new articulation (such as a hammer-on, pull-off, slide or vibrato begins, or
3. The note is a barely audible "ghost" note (note in standard notation is also in parentheses).

Hendrix Publications from Hal Leonard

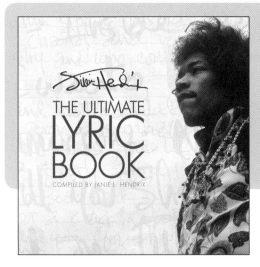

Jimi Hendrix THE ULTIMATE LYRIC BOOK

compiled by Janie L. Hendrix • Backbeat Books

Here are all of the words to the Hendrix classics you've rocked along to for years, as well as unpublished songs from "Valley of Neptune" and other hitherto undiscovered sources, gathered together. The book includes numerous examples of Jimi's handwritten lyrics, often scribbled on hotel stationary, as well as photos of Jimi to accompany every song.

00333049 Hardcover Book.. $40.00

Are You Experienced

11 songs: Are You Experienced • Foxey Lady • Hey Joe • Manic Depression • Purple Haze • The Wind Cries Mary • and more.
00692930 Guitar Recorded Versions.....................$24.95
00660097 Easy Recorded Versions $12.95
00690371 Bass Recorded Versions $17.95
00690372 Drum Recorded Versions $16.99
00672308 Transcribed Scores (17 songs) $29.95

Axis: Bold as Love

13 songs: Bold as Love • Castles Made of Sand • Little Wing • Spanish Castle Magic • and more.
00692931 Guitar Recorded Versions $22.95
00672345 Transcribed Scores $29.95

Band of Gypsys

Contains note-for-note transcriptions of: Who Knows • Machine Gun • Changes • Power to Love • Message of Love • We Gotta Live Together. Includes introduction and playing tips.
00690304 Guitar Recorded Versions $24.99
00672313 Transcribed Scores $29.95

Blue Wild Angel

All 18 songs from *Jimi Hendrix – Live at the Isle of Wright*. Includes: All Along the Watchtower • Dolly Dagger • Foxey Lady • Freedom • Machine Gun • Sgt. Pepper's Lonely Hearts Club Band • and more.
00690608 Guitar Recorded Versions $24.95

Blues

10 transcriptions of Jimi's most popular blues tunes complete with an extensive introduction and photo section: Born Under a Bad Sign • Catfish Blues • Hear My Train a Comin' • Once I Had a Woman • Red House • Voodoo Chile Blues • and more.
00694944 Guitar Recorded Versions.....................$24.95

Electric Ladyland

16 songs: All Along the Watchtower • Have You Ever Been (To Electric Ladyland) • Voodoo Child (Slight Return) • and more.
00692932 Guitar Recorded Versions $24.95

People, Hell and Angels

Matching folio to the 2013 release featuring rare recordings that Hendrix made in the late 1960s. Songs include: Bleeding Heart • Crash Landing • Earth Blues • Easy Blues • Hear My Train a Comin' • Hey Gypsy Boy • Inside Out • Izabella • Let Me Move You • Mojo Man • Somewhere • Villanova Junction.
00119619 Guitar Recorded Versions....................$22.99

Smash Hits

Hendrix's 1969 best-of compilation of 12 songs: All Along the Watchtower • Crosstown Traffic • Fire • Foxey Lady • Hey Joe • Purple Haze • Remember • Stone Free • The Wind Cries Mary.
00690602 Guitar Recorded Versions.....................$24.99
00699723 Guitar Play-Along.................................$19.95
00699835 Drum Play-Along.................................$16.95

West Coast Seattle Boy:
The Jimi Hendrix Anthology

Here are more than 30 tracks from the boxed set of previously unreleased studio and live recordings: Castles Made of Sand • Fire • Hear My Train a Comin' (Get My Heart Back Together) • The New Rising Sun • 1983...(A Merman I Should Turn to Be) • Purple Haze • Star Spangled Banner • The Wind Cries Mary • and more.
00691152 Guitar Recorded Versions.....................$29.99

Winterland (Highlights)

This folio transcribes every note as Hendrix played them on 11 songs from the live recordings of his performances at San Francisco's Winterland Ballroom in 1968. Includes: Are You Experienced? • Fire • Foxey Lady • Hey Joe • Little Wing • Manic Depression • Voodoo Child (Slight Return) • and more.
00691332 Guitar Recorded Versions.....................$22.99

Live at Woodstock

Relive Hendrix's Woodstock performance with these 11 songs: Red House • Star Spangled Banner • Villanova Junction • and more. Includes photos.
00690017 Guitar Recorded Versions $24.95

Experience Hendrix – Book One
Beginning Guitar Method

by Michael Johnson

This step-by-step process of learning music using the songs of Jimi Hendrix teaches guitar basics, music basics, music/guitar theory, scales, chords, reading music, guidelines for practicing, tips on caring for your guitar, and much more.
00695159 Book/CD Pack.....................................$14.95

Jimi Hendrix – Experience Hendrix

20 of Hendrix's best: All Along the Watchtower • Bold as Love • Castles Made of Sand • Foxey Lady • Hey Joe • Manic Depression • Purple Haze • Star Spangled Banner • The Wind Cries Mary • and more.
00672397 Transcribed Scores $29.95
00307009 Piano/Vocal/Guitar $16.95

In Deep with Jimi Hendrix

by Andy Aledort

This book breaks down and reassembles the solos, riffs, rhythm figures, harmony lines, ensemble parts, and more from over 40 of Hendrix' greatest songs.
00660335 Guitar School $19.95

Play like Jimi Hendrix

by Andy Aledort

This comprehensive book and audio teaching method provides detailed analysis of Hendrix's gear, tone, techniques, styles, songs, licks, riffs, and much more. Songs include: All Along the Watchtower • Bold As Love • Foxey Lady • Hey Joe • Purple Haze • The Wind Cries Mary • and more.
00127586 Book/Online Audio..............................$19.99

Jimi Hendrix – Signature Licks

by Andy Aledort

Performance notes, chord voicings, scale use, and unusual techniques are included for 12 songs: Foxey Lady • Hey Joe • Little Wing • Purple Haze • and more.
00696560 Book/Online Audio..............................$24.95

Jimi Hendrix – Learn to Play the
Songs from Are You Experienced

This DVD shows guitarists how to play parts of every song on this album. Songs: Purple Haze • Love or Confusion • The Wind Cries Mary • Fire • Third Stone from the Sun • Can You See Me • and more.
00320274 DVD $59.95

Prices, contents, and availability subject to change without notice.

Study the master with these transcriptions and explorations of the techniques and tunes that made Hendrix a legend.

7777 W. BLUEMOUND RD. P.O. BOX 13819 MILWAUKEE, WI 53213
Complete song lists online at
www.halleonard.com

0316